D1736435

How to Finance
100% of Your
Real Estate Sales

Also by the Author

30-Day Accelerated Training Program for Real Estate Sales People

How to Finance 100% of Your Real Estate Sales

Larry L. Sandifar

PRENTICE-HALL, INC.
ENGLEWOOD CLIFFS, NEW JERSEY

Prentice-Hall International, Inc., *London*
Prentice-Hall of Australia, Pty. Ltd., *Sydney*
Prentice-Hall of Canada, Ltd., *Toronto*
Prentice-Hall of India Private Ltd., *New Delhi*
Prentice-Hall of Japan, Inc., *Tokyo*
Prentice-Hall of Southeast Asia Pte. Ltd., *Singapore*
Whitehall Books, Ltd., *Wellington, New Zealand*

Library of Congress Cataloging in Publication Data

Sandifar, Larry L
    How to finance 100% of your real estate sales.

    Includes index.
    1. Real estate business--Finance.   I. Title.
HD1375.S256   333.33'068'1   80-29446
ISBN 0-13-406603-0

Dedication

To my mother, Jean Cogan, whose unselfish acts and teachings have enabled me to not only succeed in life, but also to enjoy life. If I could have chosen anyone in the world for a mother, I would have chosen her. If I can be as good a parent, my children will be extremely fortunate.

Acknowledgments

As a writer, my contribution to this book has been to put the thoughts down on paper and report the success of your peers in the real estate industry. Many others, without whom this book would not have been possible, have contributed much more.

In particular, I would like to express my sincere and deepest appreciation to three individuals whose efforts have made this book one that you, the reader, can use to increase your success in financing real estate:

Cindy Misner, for her excellent and untiring editorial advice and creative ideas. Without her, I would not have been able to achieve my goal of providing you with a complete and well-written book on financing.

Walter Straub and Steve Perry of Waterfield Mortgage Co. for their expert advice and tremendous insight on how to overcome the problems of financing real estate.

The value of the support and assistance given by these individuals cannot be measured fully by anyone other than myself. Thank you.

How This Book
Can Help You Finance
100% of Your
Real Estate Sales

How many commissions did you lose in the past six months because you could not obtain financing? How many buyers did you pass up because you felt they wouldn't qualify to buy a home? Two? Ten? Twenty?

Your answer should be ZERO. When you have devoted your time, effort and selling expertise, and finally beat out the competition for your buyer, you should *never* lose a commission because of lack of financing. Financing is a key factor in selling real estate that you *can* control, and one of the few areas that allows you the flexibility to use dozens of different avenues to succeed.

How to Finance 100% of Your Real Estate Sales will give you the ability to ensure that never never again will you lose a big commission because of financing problems. Not only are you presented with over 30 different methods of financing and 16 different financing outlets, but you are also presented with creative and proven techniques for using these financing sources to solve any financing problem.

This book shows you how to use every financing avenue available, many of which you may not have even known existed. You'll learn how to qualify the buyer, how to improve the appraisal value of the property, how to match up buyers and financing, how to improve your buyer's credit and income picture, how to successfully appeal rejected loans or low appraisals, where to find mortgage and down payment money and how to use financing to attract buyers and sell real estate.

In *How to Finance 100% of Your Real Estate Sales,* you'll learn new and more effective ways to use:

- FHA (Over 15 different avenues)
- VA
- Secondary Mortgage Markets such as pledges, second mortgages, notes, private lenders, equity loans, outside collateral for loans and more.
- Investment property financing
- Leases
- Chattels
- Small Business Administration
- Contracts and Assumptions
- Package Mortgages
- Conventional loans
- Blanket Mortgages
- Farm loans
- Purchase Money Mortgages
- Construction loans
- Bare land financing
- plus 15 other profitable methods of financing real estate sales.

Once you discover that all buyers can be financed, you'll increase your list of clientele manyfold. Every call-in will be a hot prospect. Everyone you contact will be a potential buyer. You'll also discover that prospects will be less selective in their choice of homes because they are buying the financing as much as they are the home.

Here are just a few of the many examples included in this book that can show you how to use creative and aggressive financing as others have to collect commissions on seemingly hopeless transactions.

- How a buyer who had declared bankruptcy was financed into a $40,000 home.
- How a buyer with poor credit and delinquent payments was guided so that he eventually qualified for a loan.
- How four different businesses were financed, even though the buyers had small down payments.
- How three methods of financing were used to close a loan.
- How a commercial building was financed through VA.
- How a rejection was turned into a closing after both the buyer and the property had been turned down.

- How contracts were used to obtain 100% financing and still release the seller's equity.
- How the staff of an entire office increased their earnings dramatically by applying the financing techniques included in this book.
- How a client's income picture was easily and quickly improved to qualify her for a loan.
- How an unmarried couple was financed on VA by getting both of their incomes counted.
- Much, much more. In each of the 30-plus methods of financing discussed, you are given examples of effective, tested techniques that can be used to make financing work for you.

Financing your real estate sales requires more knowledge and aggressiveness than any other aspect of your selling process, yet for most, it is the least developed skill and the least pursued aspect of your real estate business. A real estate agent will stick with a buyer or seller, regardless of the number of negative responses he gets, until he gets the offer signed. Yet, when a lending officer says "no," the agent throws the offer in the waste basket.

Financing is no different from selling. You stick with it until you get the job done. Every time you run into an objection, you can overcome it—by following the guidelines in this book. There is always a financing method available to you and a firm or individual that wants to lend your client the money he or she needs. *How to Finance 100% of Your Real Estate Sales* will show you how to find that individual and that method.

How successful are these aggressive and creative financing techniques? In many years of experience as a real estate salesman, sales manager, and financing consultant, I have lost only two closings because of financing, and in each case the reason was the buyer's unwillingness to follow through on the action he should have taken to have the loan approved. The secrets of the art of financing and the creativity I used to compile this record are all contained in the following pages. Many of my clients have doubled or tripled their incomes by using these unusual, highly effective techniques. By employing the detailed procedures you are given in this book, you, too, can finance *100% of your real estate sales.*

Larry L. Sandifar

Contents

Chapter Three – An FHA or VA Loan for Your Every Need

Chapter Four – VA Financing: an Untapped Market

Chapter Five – Financing Business and Commercial Property

CHAPTER ONE

Successful Financing
is an Attitude,
Not an Ability

The secret to successful financing lies more in the attitude you possess than in the knowledge you possess. Each transaction has its own peculiarities that need to be considered when searching for mortgage funds. The buyer's income, credit standing, assets and monthly obligations will be different from the last client you dealt with. Even the home will have different characteristics that will have to be considered. It is impossible to have all the knowledge of what can be done in every situation, because in many cases the package you put together will be unique to that transaction. Only a positive, aggressive and open-minded attitude towards financing will enable you to excel at developing outlets designed to meet your clients' needs.

Too many real estate agents, both experienced and beginners, make the mistake of trying to find prospects who meet standards for financing avenues they are familiar with. This limits their field of prospects and puts the agent into competition with every other agent in town. Within legal limits, anyone can purchase a home. The successful agent understands this fact and approaches every prospect with the confidence that he has the ability to find an avenue that will meet the buyer's needs.

There are hundreds of couples in your community who would love to own a home, but have been told they cannot. They can; and any real estate agent who tells them they can't, simply because he doesn't know how to finance them, is doing the prospect a disservice, and is losing a commission for himself.

ANYONE CAN PURCHASE A HOME, BUT NOT EVERY AGENT CAN SELL IT

As a real estate agent who has passed up prospects or lost transactions because of the rejection of the buyer by the lender, you may not want to admit this fact to be a truth; but it is. Anyone *can* purchase a home. If the final outcome of your efforts is not a commission check, YOU failed in your responsibility, not the buyer. With over 30 methods of financing and thousands of outlets for mortgage funds, only your inability to put the right package together can cause failure.

I have financed people who had filed for bankruptcy, had outstanding collections, slow credit, an unstable income, limited income, no down payment, no credit, were unmarried couples, and couples where one of the buyers was a minor. I have used horses, used cars, furniture, retirement bonds, cattle, notes, equipment and accounts receivable for collateral. I have used up to five different types of financing to close a transaction and at times had to make five or six tries before finding the right financing avenue for a buyer. I have also made a good living from financing buyers rejected by other salespeople. You will learn, as you read this book, that anyone truly can buy a home, if you will use all of the avenues and resources at your disposal to show them how.

SUCCESSFUL FINANCING: A FIVE-PART FORMULA

If you are to finance each client you work with, you must adopt the proper formula for successful financing. There are five essential ingredients for creative and effective financing:

1. Confidence in your ability to finance anyone
2. Familarity with all available financing avenues and outlets
3. Familiarity with your buyer's circumstances
4. Matching your buyer with the right property
5. Getting a commitment from your buyer

Part 1: Confidence in Your Ability to Finance Anyone

Too often we feel we can do only what has succeeded before or what someone else has told us we can do. Even though this book contains dozens of examples of techniques that have been developed to finance buyers and gives you guidelines for many different types and sources of financing, it is by no means a complete list of what you can do. That's what makes financing exciting. Each transaction is different, and each requires your creativity to make it work.

The most important factor is your own confidence in your ability. If you know there is an answer, you will stick with the transaction until you find the solution. The answer is always there if you have enough determination to find it. If some people did not have faith in their ability to attack new areas, we wouldn't have the light bulb, the automobile, penicillin, or the airplane. Edison, Ford, Pasteur, the Wright Brothers and thousands of others to whom we owe our rich lives had the confidence to continue until they found the answer for which they were searching. Don't ask if something CAN be done or if it HAS been done; ask why CAN'T it be done or why WON'T it work. Most of my commissions have come from transactions my peers or lenders said couldn't be closed. They couldn't close them because they didn't think they could. I closed them because I knew I could.

Part 2: Familarity with all Available Financing Avenues and Outlets

To not be aware of a financing avenue or outlet is to pass up an opportunity to earn a commission check. Every avenue and outlet is beneficial to you and each increases your chances to earn a commission. I have found that when an agent condemns a particular method of financing, it is because he does not know enough about it to make it work for him.

When I took my first job as a sales manager, I was amazed at how little my agents knew about financing. We were the fourteenth largest office in our area and not a single salesperson was earning in excess of $10,000 per year. After introducing them to the many dif-

ferent facets of real estate financing and changing their attitudes
about the flexibility of financing, our sales soared. Within one year
we jumped to become the fourth largest office with each agent
more than doubling his income. Because of our success, we were then
able to attract salespeople from other offices. All this was attributed
to our agents' becoming aware of the need to sell financing, as well
as houses.

How can you become familiar with every financing avenue and
outlet? First, by finishing this book. Second, by reviewing previous
closings in your office, taking note of any creative financing techniques employed. And third, by getting out and talking to your local
lenders, finance companies, mortgage companies, SBA officials,
FHA and VA officials, insurance companies, and lease companies.
Ask questions and give examples. Get any brochures they have available. In other words, utilize their services and knowledge. And last,
but not least, try new techniques. You can't possibly know if something will or won't work until you try it.

Part 3: Familiarity with Your Buyer's Circumstances

One of the biggest mistakes made by many agents is their failure
to know everything about their buyers. You can never assume anything and even what might seem to be of least importance can cause
a loan application to be rejected. Likewise, something that the buyer
considers to be unimportant or takes for granted, might be just what
you need to get the loan approved.

Qualify every buyer immediately. Before you ever start showing
him houses, you have to know what you will have to do to get him
financed. If your buyer has to buy on contract, FHA, VA, or will need
a pledge or second mortgage from the seller, you will have to select
homes that fit the buyer's needs. If your buyer has a credit problem,
is overextended, or is short on income or down payment, you can't
wait until you get to the loan application to find out you have a
problem.

When you sit down with your buyer for the qualifying session,
anticipate problem areas and ask leading questions that will indicate
whether there are any problems without making your buyer feel you
are judging him. The point you have to make is that you will find
him a house, and that you can finance anyone, but to do so you must
have a complete picture of what conditions or problems you will have
to take into consideration.

Always run at least an oral credit report on your buyers. Not only will they sometimes be less than completely honest with you, but many times they may not be aware of something that shows on their report. The cost is nominal considering the problems it can save you down the road.

I once had an agent who lost a sale because he assumed his buyers had sufficient credit, income and down payment for a home in the price range in which they were looking. After two weeks of running them all over town, they bought a home for $20,000 less than the homes this agent had been showing them. Since he had assumed they could qualify for the homes in the price range they had told him they wanted to buy, the buyers were too embarrassed to tell him they couldn't. Their only graceful way out was to go to someone else to buy a home. Most buyers have a problem of some sort. Find your buyer's problem, before it costs you a commission and your buyers a home.

Part 4: Matching Your Buyer with the Right Property

Of course, your success is always dependent upon matching your buyer with the right property, but for purposes of financing, this requirement is more difficult and less obvious than just finding the home your buyer likes. For instance, your buyer wants a three-bedroom home on the west side of town in the $40,000 price range. You find six homes that meet the description and show each of them to your client. Your buyer likes house No. 5 and wants to make an offer using FHA terms. Unaware of your buyer's need to buy through FHA, you showed him house No. 5 knowing that it couldn't be sold through FHA. Your problem now is that not only have you wasted time, but you have your buyer's heart set on a home he can't buy.

If your client's needs are to buy on contract, you have to limit your showings to those homes that will sell on contract. The same holds true for FHA, VA, assumption, secondary financing, qualifications for monthly payment, etc. Many buyers will purchase a home solely because it is the best one you can get financed for them. In other words, they buy the terms as much as or more than the home.

Part 5: Getting a Commitment from Your Buyer

Once you are familiar with your buyer's circumstances and have determined what must be done to get your buyer financed, you must get a commitment from him to do what is required to get the transaction closed. You should make the buyer aware from the very beginning of what he must do to obtain a home. He may have to clear up some old debts, write letters of explanation, raise additional funds or settle for less than his dream house. He may have to stick with you for several weeks to give you time to get an approval. Regardless of your needs, your buyer must be willing to do his part to help you succeed at getting the transaction closed. If your buyer isn't committed to the same goal you are, you'll never earn the commission.

LEARNING TO BE AS AGGRESSIVE IN FINANCING AS YOU ARE IN SELLING

To succeed at financing 100% of your offers, you have to approach this aspect of the transaction with the same type of aggressiveness as you use to get the offer. You can't take "no" for an answer or fail to attempt to use every avenue available to you. The best example I can give you is your own experience. Think back to the last time a buyer said "no" to you. What did you do? Did you say "Gee, that's too bad," and go find another buyer? Of course not. You stuck with him, overcame his objections and, if necessary, you found a different home for him, right?

Now, think back to the last time a lending officer rejected your buyer's application. What did you do? You probably said, "Gee, that's too bad," threw the offer away and started looking for new clients. Why? Why would you throw out all of that work when you had already done the hard part? You had a willing buyer and seller, and just because one person, a person who really has nothing to lose, says "no," you toss out the whole transaction.

Let's back up for a moment. If you look at your attitude when soliciting an offer and apply this same attitude towards financing, you will achieve the same result. Sooner or later, you will get a "yes," but if you don't care enough to put in some work, the lender won't care enough either. If you get a rejection, find out why. Is there anything you could do that would put the application in a different light? Are there any conditions under which the lender would accept the application? What do you need to correct before going to another lender? Is there another avenue you should pursue where the problem your buyer has would be accepted?

There is a source of funds for everyone. There are thousands of private, public, and government outlets begging to loan money. If you are aggressive enough, you will find the right one for your buyer.

FINANCING CREATIVITY PAYS OFF IN COMMISSIONS

Unless you are willing to base your income on the successes of others or on what a conservative banker tells you is possible, you must put creativity into your financing efforts. There are no set, diehard rules to follow when financing a buyer and property. There are some guidelines that will make your job easier and that will give you some shortcuts. What I hope to do in the remaining chapters is to give you some ideas that will get your creative juices flowing.

Each time you come up with a new idea, or develop a new technique, you have earned a commission that would have otherwise been lost. Not only does your income depend on your creativity, but whether your buyers can get the home they want or not also depends on how creative you are. How much difference can your individual efforts and creativity mean? They can mean the difference between a closing and a rejection. Only you and your abilities can bridge the gap between these points in many cases.

TURNING CREATIVE IDEAS INTO BIG DOLLARS

We had a property listed that offered one of the most beautiful lots in the area. Once used as a lodge, the site offered hundred-year-old trees, four outside barbeque pits, a large stream, and was nestled between some very beautiful and expensive homes. The lodge itself, however, had been gutted by a fire and required complete remodeling, plus some structural changes to make it suitable for a home. The owner was not willing to sell on contract and the banks would not loan over 50% on the property.

One of my agents had a VA buyer interested in the property, but the VA wouldn't loan money on the home in its present condition. Using his creative talents, the salesman put together a successful formula to close the offer. He presented the VA with a loan application and requested an appraisal based on the plans for remodeling the home which were submitted with the application. The VA then issued a commitment for a loan to be made after the remodeling was completed. With this commitment in hand, he then arranged short-term financing for the purchase and remodeling of the property.

While none of these methods alone, or as they would normally be used, could have been successful, by combining them and using some variations, the salesman earned a $1400 commission check.

DESIGNING NEW METHODS AND TECHNIQUES FOR FINANCING BUYERS

You cannot depend on yesterday's accomplishments to get you through today. Each day presents new challenges and requires you to devise new financing methods and techniques to meet these challenges. Your last transaction will be completely different from your next transaction. You will never know all there is to know about financing. I have written manuals on financing, conducted seminars, and earn attractive fees for my consulting services, yet I'm constantly trying new techniques, discovering new methods and searching for new outlets. Once you convince yourself you know all there is to know, you have talked yourself into settling for less commission money than you could have earned.

The most important element in designing new and effective financing techniques is to realize that your flexibility is in the financing, and not in the buyers' abilities. Your buyers are basically saddled with their credentials, and even though you can show them how to improve the picture, you still must remain within the scope of their limits. But you can stretch, change and combine financing to meet their needs.

The following chapters will demonstrate to you just how flexible financing can be, and how others have used each method to design financing terms to fit their buyers' and sellers' needs. The most difficult habit to overcome is allowing yourself to fall into a rut. It is very easy to focus your thinking on one particular type of financing and when it fails, give up on the transaction. You have to stand back and take a broader look at your goal and at the obstacles standing in your way. Many times, discussing your problem with an associate will help. I use an easel to list both the assets available to me and the obstacles. This method allows me to get an overall picture of the situation, instead of focusing on just the obstacles.

MATCHING FINANCING AND BUYERS

The secret of successfully matching your buyer with the right financing lies in your approach to the problem. You can't take just a surface view covering the amount of down payment, credit, income and condition of property and make a correct decision on what type of financing, if any, will or will not work. You can't list the methods of financing you're familiar with and try to fit your buyer into one of those categories. Most buyers aren't perfect, so they won't conveniently fit into A, B, or C. You have to be able to take the conditions your buyer has presented you and develop financing terms that will work, using A, B or C or A, B, and C as the base from which you work. Let me give you the following example.

You have a seller who will sell through FHA and pay the points and closing costs. You have already received an FHA appraisal on the property and have secured a buyer who is looking for a home such as the one you have listed with a low down payment. You run an oral credit report and find that the buyer's credit isn't good enough to qualify for an FHA loan.

Now, the question is do you toss the buyer aside or do you develop financing terms that will give the buyer, the seller, and you what you all want? (Have you figured out the answer yet? Well, let me have the fun of telling you anyway.) Have the seller refinance his home on FHA and then allow your buyer to assume the loan. You can collect your commission from the proceeds from the refinancing and, if you have used a mortgage company, the assumption will not require a lender's approval or cost your buyer anything, except a small fee for the paperwork. The seller has sold his home, the buyer has the home he wants, and you have a well-deserved commission check that many salespeople would never have earned.

KEEPING AN OPEN MIND IN YOUR FINANCING EFFORTS

If there is anything worse than having an associate or lender tell you something isn't possible, it's your telling yourself it isn't possible. Your attitude, your commitment that you can develop new methods of financing, will ensure your success. Only when you start taking the easy way out will you begin to fail. When you say "no" to your buyer, you are also saying "no" to the commission check he is offering you.

Keeping an open mind, however, is more than just having the attitude that anything is possible. As I mentioned earlier, you must also be constantly aware that if you are running into an insurmountable obstacle with the method of financing you have selected, you can go around the obstacle by taking a new route. The more complicated the package you are putting together, the easier it is to fall into a narrow rut, forgetting other options available to you. Each new wrinkle you encounter and conquer brings you further into the depths of the transaction, until you no longer recognize the point at which you began.

There are several ways to overcome this problem. As I mentioned, I use a large easel so I can always have an overall view of my options when putting a package together. I also suggest discussing your financing problems with an associate or your broker. Another method you can use is to keep a list of every financing method along with a brief description of the circumstances under which each works best. After writing down the facts with which you have to work concerning the buyer, the seller, and the property, review each financing method and ask yourself, "Why won't this method work in this situation?" Now review your list of possibilities and select the best method for this particular transaction, keeping in mind your other options should you run into an obstacle with the method you have chosen.

Keeping an open mind also means not rejecting a financing method or technique just because it has never been tried before under the same circumstances with which you are working. The fact that it hasn't been used before doesn't mean it isn't possible. It only means that a lender hasn't had an opportunity to make a loan under the same conditions you have for him this time.

SEARCHING FOR NEW METHODS AND OUTLETS

Finding new sources for mortgage funds or new methods that can be of benefit to you in your real estate business requires constant attention. Salespeople who rely on a few outlets limit their flexibility in times of good money supply and often find themselves without mortgage outlets during periods of tight money supply.

Outlets you should always be searching for include mortgage companies, finance companies, lease companies, government agencies, private sources, and commercial lenders. These outlets may be local, area, state, or national. Don't let the fact that the source isn't local stop you from following up on it. I have used lenders located over 2,000 miles from the property being used for collateral.

You can find many outlets by reading business periodicals, visiting an abstract company, looking through distant cities' phone books, inquiring at franchise restaurants as to lease companies or national lenders, visiting the courthouse to see who now holds mortgages in your area, and contacting major insurance companies with regard to their lending policies. Federal, state and local agencies can also help you identify potential lenders, making you aware of lenders who do business with them.

Once you realize that you are not solely dependent upon your local lenders for your mortgage money supply, your potential becomes unlimited. You are also in a better position to apply pressure on the local lenders, because if you don't get what you want, you have someone else to turn to. There is absolutely no excuse for not finding funds for your buyer. Thousands of lenders spend their days trying to figure out whom to loan money to, because they know they can't make a profit if they don't loan any money. Help them out, won't you?

CHAPTER TWO

Using FHA
to Triple
Your Commissions

TURNING LEMONS INTO LEMONADE

FHA can be one of the most important avenues of financing for you as a real estate agent. If you are familiar with the ins and outs of FHA, you can finance almost anyone, regardless of age, income, length of employment, credit or marital status.

FHA has a bad name among many real estate salespeople because they lack the knowledge to make FHA work for them. By studying this chapter, you will gain the knowledge you need to make FHA work for you. Your transactions will go smoother, faster, and be approved with more regularity than ever before.

How many people do you know who would like to buy a house but feel they can't because of down payment requirements, income, credit, marital status, past bankruptcy, etc.? Your answer will be probably more people than those who do have money and credit. For most of these prospects, FHA can be the answer to your financing problems. FHA offers more flexibility and more programs than any other type of financing.

The most attractive aspect to FHA buyers is that they will purchase a home any time of the year. Usually they are buying their first home and they don't really care what the weather or economy is like. They are also purchasing financing terms and will be extremely loyal to the agent who will show them how they can get into a home of their own.

UNDERSTANDING HOUSING REQUIREMENTS FOR FHA LOANS AND PUTTING THEM TO WORK FOR YOU

Do not confuse FHA and VA house requirements. There are many differences in these two loans. In many cases, if you know these differences in advance, it will help you decide which is the best avenue for a particular property. FHA has generally stricter requirements concerning the home. Neither of these agencies redlines, which makes them the only way to finance many properties. (Redlining, for those unfamiliar with the term, is a lending institution's decision that it will not loan money on property in a certain area. It is illegal, but difficult to prove.)

MINIMUM PROPERTY STANDARDS

The property must meet minimum FHA property standards. Below is a list of major points to look for when considering a property for an FHA appraisal. It is by no means a complete list of requirements, but rather a list of areas to watch for, in order to save time in processing.

Furnace – Must be in good working order. Heating ducts are required in each room. FHA will usually not accept wall furnaces and space heaters. They are also very critical of conversion units.

Paint – All paint and trim must be in good condition. You will be better off getting any necessary painting finished prior to appraisal.

Roof and Eaves – FHA will not only look at the condition of the roof, but will also take notice of the pattern of the shingles. This tells them the age of the roof, and if it is too old, FHA will require a new one. Since FHA does not always require gutters, you will be better off with no gutters, than with ones in need of repair. They will require the roof and eaves to have proper ventilation.

Wiring – FHA will require 100-amp wiring on larger homes. Smaller homes can usually get by with 60-amp wiring. Two separate and remote outlets or one outlet and one light fixture in each habitable room are also required. A kitchen must have three outlets and a bathroom and basement must have at least one outlet each. All obsolete wiring must be removed and replaced with new wiring. No wiring should be exposed.

Windows – All glass must be without cracks or holes. Windows must all be in operating condition. Caulking must be tight and all handles must be in place on doors and windows.

Insulation – FHA requires a minimum of 6 inches of insulation in the attic, including knee wells. The attic area must be properly ventilated.

Garage – FHA will be fairly demanding about the garage. If it is badly in need of repair, you will be better off tearing it down before appraisal.

Septic and Well – You may be required to have the well and septic system certified. If you are, your County Health Department will be happy to make the necessary tests and supply you with certification.

Basement – FHA will require the basement to be reasonably dry. If they see an indication of dampness, they will require the sealing of basement walls.

Landscaping – FHA will look at the drainage and require it to be adequate according to their standards.

LENDING LIMITS UNDER FHA

If the house is less than one year old, it must have been built under FHA specifications. The maximum allowable mortgage amounts of FHA 203B loans, (normal FHA) are as follows:

One Unit	$60,000
Two and Three Units	$65,000
Four Units	$75,000

If income is tight, too much or too little house may be reason for rejection. On older homes the appraiser may also reduce the economic life of the house, thereby reducing the number of years on the life of the loan, and raising the payment for which your buyer must qualify. If in doubt about the number of years you can expect to get on a house because of its condition, protect yourself by making sure your buyer can qualify for a larger monthly payment. The appraiser will also estimate the utilities, taxes, insurance, and maintenance on the home; and his estimate will generally be higher than the actual figures. The unfortunate part is that your buyer will have to qualify under the appraiser's estimated figures, rather than under the actual amount he'll be paying. This means you must leave yourself room, when qualifying your buyer, for a higher utility estimate than the actual figures would indicate.

SECURING A STRONG APPRAISAL FROM FHA

If you are securing an appraisal on a vacant home, send the key with the appraisal request. If the home is occupied, go with the appraiser to see that he does not have difficulty getting in, has no problems with tenants, or trouble with pets. There is nothing worse than having the man who will decide whether your house will pass or not be made uncomfortable. Help him measure and answer his questions. Make his inspection a smooth one.

When filling out the appraisal request, don't list items such as draperies, curtains, appliances, air conditioners, etc. FHA will deduct the value of these items from the appraisal. If you are getting an advance appraisal in hopes of selling the home FHA, it will not hurt to ask for more than you need. Leave yourself some room for the appraiser to cut the price, for points to raise or pay for repairs. If none of these things occurs, you can sell the home for less than the appraised value. Don't do this all the time, however. FHA may get wise if they see offers consistently coming in for lower than the appraised value.

FINANCING YOUR BUYER'S CLOSING COSTS

If for some reason you should get the loan amount cut, or need to get more money, you can add the estimated closing costs to the mortgage amount. You must say the buyer is financing his closing costs. For instance, let's assume you have an appraisal on a property for $35,500. We know that the normal FHA mortgage would be for $34,200. The appraisal will show, however, that the estimated closing costs are $750 and that the maximum mortgage is $34,950. You can actually get a higher loan and increase your seller's net. This has saved several transactions for me when the price was cut, or repairs were ordered that neither the buyer nor the seller could afford to pay for.

If your appraisal is short, and the buyer wishes, he may pay more for the home. The difference between the purchase price and appraised value must be paid in cash. You will save yourself time and get a better appraisal if the work you know will be required is finished before the appraiser arrives. A home sells better when in good repair and it also appraises better. If a reinspection is required, you will lose anywhere from one to two weeks waiting for the closing.

The only real advantage to getting an appraisal before you receive an offer on the property is to let you know what you have to work with. If you know the terms FHA will issue, you can advertise them and the seller will be prepared for an FHA offer. It usually does not speed up the process. An appraisal is good for six months and can be extended for six months for a $25 fee. The original appraisal costs $60. FHA does not charge more for an apartment building or new home. Neither do they charge a reinspection fee, as VA does. If it is necessary to have a reinspection after repairs, it will be done by someone other than the appraiser.

APPEALING AN FHA APPRAISAL

Unlike most conventional loan appraisals, an FHA appraisal can be appealed. As with VA appeals, all that is required is for you to submit three *sold* comparables with your appeal. You should also attempt to counter any points that the FHA appraiser felt were negative. FHA appraisers are FHA employees. They have superiors who review their appraisals and someone with more authority who will consider your appeal. Since you are questioning the work of their employees, however, and not just of a contract appraiser, they are not as likely as VA to give you a new appraisal. Your argument will have to be a strong one.

CONDITIONING YOUR SELLER FOR AN FHA OFFER

You know that certain price ranges and locations will likely sell FHA. FHA allows the home to sell more quickly and for a better price. The best opportunity you have to make the owner aware of this is when you are giving your listing presentation. This allows you to make the owner aware of what is involved regarding time, points, costs and repairs. It also gives you an opportunity to build the costs involved into the listing price. You know that this is probably the only way the owner is going to sell his home, so make him aware of it and you won't have an irate seller on your hands when you surprise him with an FHA offer. I always assume the seller will have to pay all closing costs. By doing this and making the owner aware of what they are, I have paved the way for any offer.

If it happens that the buyer does have a little money, my seller won't mind netting more than I told him he would. You can also advertise the home more effectively if you can use the point that your seller will pay these costs. The important part of making any type of financing work is to anticipate the worst. Most serious problems are caused by the salesperson not anticipating difficulties and not communicating with the seller. Work on those two areas and your closings will go much more smoothly.

Most modern homes, regardless of age, will meet the minimum property standards set forth by FHA. New homes built under FHA understandably qualify. New homes not built under FHA qualify; however, the loan amount is reduced to 90 percent of the first $35,000.

Down Payment Requirements

First $25,000   97% insurable or 3% down
Over $25,000   95% insurable or 5% down

Example

$38,900 sales price – Maximum allowable mortgage amount with seller paying closing costs:

First $25,000 $ 750 down
Next $13,900 $ 695 down
                       $1,445 down, rounded to next highest
                                $50. Total down: $1450.

If you have a client refinancing his property under FHA, he must have his former FHA loan paid down to less than 85%.

ACQUIRING DOWN PAYMENT FUNDS FOR FHA

A buyer cannot borrow his down payment and it cannot be paid by the seller. It can come in the form of a gift, the sale of an asset, cash saved, a forthcoming tax return, a bonus, or show up as earnest money on the offer to purchase. Whatever means your client uses to obtain his down payment, it is important to know where it is coming from before application. No new loans should show up on the buyer's credit report when turned into FHA. FHA will automatically think he has borrowed his down payment. (Now buyers must even sign a statement at closing warranting that their credit, income, etc., has not changed since their loan application.)

A good way of acquiring down payment money is to have a parent give the buyers the down payment. Sometimes the parent may have to borrow the money to give his son or daughter a gift, which is not against FHA guidelines. There are many legal ways to protect yourself and find the down payment money for the buyer at the same time.

CLOSING COSTS WITH FHA AND WHO PAYS THEM

Closing costs on an FHA loan with a mortgage company will include the appraisal, title insurance, title examination, credit and photos, survey, origination fee, points and recording fees. Either the buyer or seller can pay these costs, but the seller has to pay the discount points. The seller cannot pay the prepaid items on an FHA loan. Prepaid items are the first year's insurance, two months' FHA insurance premium, two months' home owner's insurance for escrow, two months' taxes and interest from the date of closing until the end of the month. The amounts for these costs will vary, so check with your mortgage company for the costs in your area.

QUALIFYING THE BUYER

An FHA loan is available to anyone who is creditworthy, eighteen years of age or older, single, married, divorced, or living together and with an adequate income. The following method is standard for qualifying the income of FHA buyers: (Use the Worksheet on page 37.)

INCOME REQUIREMENTS FOR FHA AND HOW YOU CAN IMPROVE YOUR CLIENT'S STATUS TO MEET THEM

The worksheet following will tell you if your buyer qualifies for the FHA loan you need. Income that may be used for FHA purposes includes anything that you can verify. Some examples are rent (including the income from the property being purchased), pension,

FHA QUALIFYING WORKSHEET

1. Gross monthly income............................. ——————————
2. Federal Withholding tax........................... ——————————
3. Net monthly income.............................. ⬜
4. Principal and interest............................. ——————————
5. Mortgage insurance premium................ ——————————
6. Maintenance and utilities........................ ——————————
7. Monthly hazard insurance...................... ——————————
8. Property tax.. ——————————
9. Total housing expense........................... ⬜
10. 35% of net monthly income.................... ⬜
11. State and local taxes............................. ——————————
12. Social Security.................................... ——————————
13. Place recurring debts here..................... ——————————
14. Total monthly debt structure.................. ⬜
15. 50% of net monthly income.................... ⬜

1. Compute gross monthly income and place on line 1.
2. Subtract Federal Withholding (2) to arrive at net income. Place in block 3.
3. Compute principal and interest only on proposed loan. Place on line 4.
4. Compute mortgage insurance premium (.005 × mortgage). Place on line 5.
5. Take estimated monthly expense for maintenance and utilities. Place on line 6.
6. Place estimated monthly hazard insurance premium on line 7.
7. Compute monthly property tax payment. Place on line 8.
8. Place total of lines 4, 5, 6, 7, and 8 in block 9.
9. Place 35% of block 3 in block 10. Block 9 cannot exceed block 10.
10. Compute monthly state and local taxes (charts available from most mortgage companies). Place on line 11.
11. Compute monthly Social Security payment (6.76 × gross monthly income; 8.10 if self-employed), and place on line 12.
12. Compute total monthly debts exceeding 12 months in duration, alimony and child support. Place on line 13.
13. Place total of block 9 and lines 11, 12, and 13 in block 14.
14. Place 50% of block 3 in block 15. Block 14 cannot exceed block 15.
15. If applicant qualified in blocks 9 and 10 and 14 and 15, he qualifies financially for FHA.

trust funds, social security, welfare subsidy payments, full-time
wages, part-time wages, overtime pay, bonuses, commissions,
spouse's income, babysitting, alimony, child support, disability income or income from property sold on contract. All income must be
verified by intent to rent letters, employment verifications, court
records, bank letters, copies of contracts, etc. FHA may count only
part or none of certain types of income, if they feel it is not of a
steady nature.

The stronger the verification, the better chance you have of getting the income counted. Any employment of over six months duration should be good enough for FHA to count. If it has been less than
that, relating the buyer's present job to his past experience and a
verification showing he is free from probable layoff will improve your
chances of getting the loan approved. A statement by the employer
on the verification saying the employee is reliable and an asset to the
company will help. If you happen to know someone in the Personnel
Department, it will help for you to call and tell him what you need.
If not, have your client speak to Personnel, tell them the verification
is forthcoming and what he needs.

IMPROVING A BUYER'S INCOME PICTURE

A divorcee, 21 years old, came to me and asked me to show her
some houses. She had no money, but her mother was willing to give
her $600 to use as a down payment. She felt she could get another
$250 by saving her salary between now and the closing. She was
making $185 per week and was getting $15 per week child support.
The support was not actually coming in steadily, but we could count
on it as income. She was looking for a two-bedroom home in a good
location.

Considering the amount of down payment she had and the
monthly payments she could afford, we had to look in the $25,000
price range. I was lucky and found her a home within a few days. The
offer was written for the seller to pay all closing costs, except prepaids. My buyer was going to put $750 down ($25,000 home) and
prepaids would run about $100 if we did not have to close at the first
of the month.

We made application and ordered the appraisal. Now we had to
go to work on our income and credit. She had very little credit in her
own name, because of her age. We got a letter stating that the loan
on her car was in her dad's name, but titled to her, and she was
making the payments. We got a letter from her health spa showing
that she had had an account with them in the past and had paid on

time. We also got a letter from a furniture company where she once had a lay-away account.

We were coming out short on her income, so we got a letter from her employer, along with a good verification of employment, showing that she was due for a raise within a short time and was working several hours a week overtime. We could use her support payments for income and turned them in without a copy of the payment record, since her ex-husband's record of payment had not been good. Because he was unemployed, his support payments were not made on time.

We also obtained a letter from her landlady stating that she was a good tenant, paid her rent on time and was paying $195 per month. This did two things for us. It proved she was capable of maintaining a household of her own without a husband and that she was paying nearly the same rent that she would be paying on the house she was buying. I then had her write a letter saying that she was making a good life for her son, was maintaining a household and that she wanted to own a home for the security of her son whom she had to raise alone.

FHA called the mortgage company and requested verification of the support payments. This was good and bad. It meant they were leaning towards approving the loan or they wouldn't go to the trouble of requesting additional information; however, the payment record was not good, and if the approval depended on it, we were in trouble. I went to the courthouse and secured a copy of the payment record. I then got a letter from the ex-husband explaining that he had been laid off and gotten behind in his support payments, but was now back to work and making his payments. The loan was approved, even though initially the buyer did not appear to qualify for the loan.

If you are running over on income-to-debt ratio, you can improve the buyer's position by getting him to consolidate his loans or pay as many as necessary down to less than eleven months, so they won't be counted against him. If your client has a loan at his or her credit union, it may not show up on the credit report. Many people make the mistake of reporting their savings at the credit union and not their loans. If you don't want the loan to show, don't report the deposit in the savings. The loan could hurt your client's debt-income ratio more than the deposit will help.

CREATIVE AND PROVEN TECHNIQUES FOR IMPROVING YOUR BUYER'S CREDIT

Your buyer's credit must be current at the time you submit his application to FHA for review. All collections must be paid and bankruptcies should be at least two years old. (The older they are, the better your chances of approval). Letters should be written explaining the reason for any collections, slow payment, or bankruptcy. Don't use layoffs from work as a reason for your client's financial difficulties if the layoff occurred within the last few months. Recent layoffs make FHA wonder about the stability of your buyer's income. Old layoffs, illnesses, divorces, or business failures are good reasons for slow credit. The best reasons for collections are disagreement with bills, bills that an ex-wife ran up or medical expenses not covered by insurance.

The reasons you give for a bankruptcy should run along these same lines. The main idea is to show FHA that the reason for filing was not that your client was irresponsible. In all circumstances, you should show that the buyer has cleared up the problem, as well as the reason for it. If your buyer is behind in his payments, a consolidation loan might be a way to bring him up-to-date and reduce his total monthly outlay at the same time. Running an oral credit check before obtaining an offer from your buyer will give you time to correct his credit if necessary, and give you advance warning of any problems.

USING LETTERS TO EXPLAIN AWAY PROBLEMS

If the credit report shows no credit for your buyer, or slow credit, it will be necessary for you to obtain three good credit letters. These can come from your client's landlord, his gas station, grocery store, or stores where he has had lay-aways, or friends from whom he has borrowed money. Even if he paid cash for an item, he paid as agreed. At the end of this chapter, you will find examples of letters that can be written to improve your buyer's application. Your letters should be logical, sincere, written from your client's point of view and addressed to the mortgage officer you are dealing with.

Your client or his references must sign the letters, so they will not be hearsay. If in the last month or so your buyer has received a loan that shows up on a credit report, FHA will think it is for the down payment. It will be necessary for you to get a letter from the lender stating that the loan was not used for the down payment and giving the reason for the loan. That's why it is better if your buyer borrows no money until after the credit report has been issued. His income-to-debt ratio will be better also, if he waits.

WRITING A WINNING FHA OFFER

FHA requires the original copy of the offer to purchase with the original signatures of the buyers and sellers. It is a good idea to show your earnest money in a large enough amount to cover the down payment and the closing costs or prepaids that the buyer will have. This will end any question of where the down payment money is coming from. Take the time to make sure your earnest money, down payment and loan amount make sense.

The offer to purchase should be neat and not show any counter proposals. If it is necessary to get counters on the offer, retype the form before sending it to FHA. I made the mistake of forwarding a countered offer only once, and received a commitment for the amount of the first offer. Spell out the number of years involved in the loan, the interest rate the buyer wants, the monthly payments and the type of loan you are going to secure. Never list drapes, curtains, appliances, air conditioners, or any other extras on the copy of the offer to purchase that is going to FHA. As I pointed out earlier, they will deduct the value of these items from the appraised value of the property.

Never list the earnest money as a note. This defeats the idea of listing earnest money at all. If repairs are to be made on the home and the buyer wishes to list these on the offer to purchase, don't put them on the copy you are sending to FHA. Of course, it is important that you get a full price offer to enhance your chances of getting your seller to pay the points and closing costs.

PRESENTING THE FHA OFFER TO YOUR SELLERS

When you are preparing for the appointment with the sellers to present your offer, make sure you have all the information you need. Check with the mortgage company on their point quote. (I've seen it change daily.) Review the closing costs your seller is going to have to pay. Check your sources for comparable property that has been sold through FHA within the past few months in the seller's area. Make sure you fully understand what points are and how you're going to explain them to your seller. Neatly write down the closing items the buyer is asking the seller to pay and the amount for each. You will also find it useful to take along a copy of the buyer's oral credit report.

Actually, in presenting the offer you will almost follow the same procedure you would use in presenting any offer. Go after the points on the offer that you know will cause the least resistance first. If you have obtained a full price offer, explain as you hand the agreement to your sellers that the offer is for the listed price, but there are closing costs and points involved that will have to be paid out of the proceeds. This keeps them from getting the offered amount in their heads and then being set back when you give them their net figure. As you explain closing costs and points, remember that the main concern for the seller should be the net figure. Don't get caught in the trap of arguing the right or wrong of these costs. I've seen too many offers rejected because the seller disagreed with the principle of paying points to sell his home. You should explain points briefly, telling your client they are necessary to raise the rate of return on the loan, so it will sell on the money market. They cannot be paid by the buyer, so the seller must pay them.

This is where a full-priced offer can save you. You can explain that the buyer offered the full price because he was aware the seller would have these costs and these expenses are his negotiating factors, rather than a reduced price. When going over the closing costs with the seller, make the review brief; go into detail only if the seller has a question on an item. Get to the net figure as quickly as possible. That is the figure he must accept. Inform your seller of what to expect in the way of time, repairs, and costs. This will save you headaches in the weeks to come. If you feel the home will need some repairs, get the seller started on them before the appraiser arrives.

One advantage to the seller of selling FHA is that while the loan may take four to six weeks to process, it gives the seller time to find a suitable home for his family. At least if he accepts the offer, he knows the closing on his home will be within six weeks. How long might it take to close if he waits for another buyer? Tell him how the credit report on the buyer looks and that you feel you can get the loan approved. If there is some anticipated problem, make him aware of it. Don't scare him, but let him know there is some work to be done. Most important, show him you are confident. If you aren't, he won't be either.

CHOOSING A LENDER FOR YOUR FHA LOAN

FHA does not allow pre-approvals. In other words, they must review the application before an approval can be issued and the closing set. Therefore, there is no advantage to taking your loan to a savings and loan institution, or a bank, over a mortgage company except to save a few dollars on prepaids and possibly closing costs.

It does you no good, however, to save your buyer or seller $200 if you don't get the house closed. Mortgage companies have a much better record of getting loans approved than other lending institutions. They only survive if they get the loans closed. They must also handle a large volume to make a profit, because they sell the paper and work on the small percentage they receive from servicing the mortgage. Because of these factors, mortgage companies train their officers in the proper way to get a loan approved. They know whom to contact at FHA, how to write letters, how to clear up credit problems and what it takes to get a loan approved. Many times when I walk into a savings and loan with an FHA offer, they are not pleased to see me. To them, I represent a lot of paper work and red tape. When I go to a loan application session with my buyers, I want them to feel that the institution I have selected appreciates the opportunity to do business with them.

Some banks and savings and loans, however, are very aggressive in the FHA market. If you have such an institution available to you and its costs are lower, use them. Make sure your buyer is good, because they will be more selective than the mortgage company on the loans they make. When choosing a mortgage company, look for one that has a good rapport with FHA and a representative who has a good working knowledge of what can be accomplished with FHA. There have been many occasions when I had to point out to a mortgage officer what we could do with a certain buyer. There is nothing wrong with that, except that if you don't know what can be done with FHA, and the mortgage officer is not familiar with all the avenues available, the buyer may never have a chance.

A good mortgage company will also work with you on speeding up the closing when necessary. This can be done by allowing you to deliver the necessary papers to the mortgage company and back to the closing agent. There are times when this will make the difference in whether your loan closes or not. You should also look for a company that keeps a good line of communication open. If there is a new law or policy change that affects your business you should be made aware of it. If points change, you should know immediately. If there is something that you need to do on your buyer's application, you need to know quickly, not when the application is ready to be sent in for approval.

I have found it useful to work with more than one mortgage company at the same time. Good business thrives on competition. It is also wise to have more than one outlet for money in case of a money shortage. When a mortgage company fails to hold its commitment on points, I don't hesitate to point out that the reason *they* got my business instead of their competitor was the points they quoted and that I can take the rest of my business to their competitor.

If you happen to be in an area not serviced by a mortgage company, call one and tell them you would like to take applications for them in the area. They will handle the processing by mail, you will have created an outlet for your FHA money, and you will pick up a few extra dollars for yourself from the mortgage company.

FHA money is less likely to dry up than conventional money. When conventional money is high or not available, your mortgage companies almost always have funds available. They sell their loans so they are constantly getting money to put back into the market. If they have trouble selling their paper because of tight money, there are government agencies that will buy the mortgages to stimulate the market.

A good salesperson will use FHA when there is no other money available. You know you have to eat whether the market is good or bad. You can't just sit back and say, "I have to wait for more money to come into the market." Good times or bad, you still have to sell a home to make a commission.

APPEALING A LOAN REJECTION

There will be times when you will overlook a problem that keeps the loan from being approved. When this happens, you can resubmit the loan, after correcting the problem. It may take a letter, an explanation, or a better verification of some item. At times, the reviewer simply "gets up on the wrong side of the bed." If you feel the rejection is not justified, have your buyer contact his congressman or senator. A call from one of these representatives usually makes a difference.

The most important step is for you to review the package before it is sent to FHA to make sure you are covered in all areas. It would be better to delay the forwarding of the application a few days, than to wait two weeks and get a rejection. Doing your job right the first time is always easier.

I have had a good record of getting rejected loans reviewed and approved, so don't give up if an application comes back without approval the first time. Persistence pays off!

HOW A REJECTION WAS TURNED INTO A CLOSING

One day one of my salespeople brought me an offer on one of my listings. It was a full-priced offer to purchase with FHA financing. The property was a single-family home that had been made into a duplex. It was suitable for either use and the buyers intended to use it as a single-family home. The property was in reasonably good condition, but I did foresee some minor repairs. I got the $31,000 offer accepted with the seller agreeing to pay all the closing costs.

We soon discovered that the buyer had some credit problems. He had filed for bankruptcy 14 years ago, had one loan with a finance company and it was in arrears, and a past collection; but his employment verification was good and his income was adequate. We wrote a letter explaining that the bankruptcy was due to marital problems which eventually ended in divorce. We explained that his ex-wife had run up bills, spent all the money and that my client had missed work over the frustration of his family splitting up. Bankruptcy had appeared to be the only way out. The letter also explained that the collection was for a television set that was stolen and the insurance company was slow in paying off. The collection had since been paid. The delinquent payments to the loan company, we explained, were due to illness in the family that required quite an outlay of money.

The loan company rewrote the loan to bring it current. We then got a letter from the loan company stating that the loan was to pay back interest and principal on the old loan, was not for the down payment on his house, and the loan company understood the reason for the slowness in paying and felt the buyer had made an attempt to keep his payments up under the conditions. We also got a letter from the credit union at work and a letter from a fellow employee who had sold him a truck on time, so we could show some good credit.

The appraisal came back with a considerable number of needed repairs and a reduced term on the loan. It was, however, for the requested amount and the appraiser had allowed us $750 towards closing costs. This meant we could raise the loan amount, in turn raising the seller's net. The seller agreed to make the repairs if the $750 was added to the loan amount. The buyers agreed and we submitted the loan.

At that point a blunder occurred that was almost disastrous. We had submitted the appraisal as a duplex because if it was going to be a single-family home, FHA required removal of upstairs plumbing in the kitchen. We did not want to go to that expense, so we didn't submit it as a single-family residence. The mortgage officer was new and did not review the application properly before it was submitted to FHA. It was rejected for two reasons. One, the borrower no longer qualified with the reduced years on the loan and two, the new credit report that was issued when the buyer brought everything up-to-date, did not show a slowness at the finance company. The mortgage company failed to pull my letter explaining why the account was slow, after it did not show up. The only evidence FHA had of knowing the account had been slow was my letter. As far as the income was concerned, the loan should never have been submitted until the income-to-debt ratio was within FHA guidelines.

We still had the income from the duplex that we could turn in. I asked the mortgage company to resubmit the application with the following material: (1) an intent to rent letter showing additional income from the apartment, (2) a letter clearing up the matter with the loan company and (3) a letter from them stating that they had made a mistake in not submitting this information with the original application and the buyer should not suffer because of their clerical errors.

The second application came back approved. I notified the mortgage company and closing agent that the closing costs were to be added to the loan amount and we closed the loan.

Because of its location, this property would not have sold if not for FHA, unless the price was reduced to make it a steal. The buyer would definitely not have been able to finance a property if not for FHA and the help of someone who had a good working knowledge of FHA.

Don't give up when problems arise. There are many ways to turn a rejection into a closing. There are a few people who have to buy on contract or assumption because of their poor credit, but most can be shaped up to qualify for FHA. It may take some time, but unless you are making $50,000 per year, you have time.

FHA ACQUIRED HOMES

FHA will usually have properties in all areas that they have repossessed. They make these homes available to the public at an advertised price, and encourage anyone interested in them to contact their broker. FHA likes to have someone coordinating the sale and does not mind paying a commission, since it's the people's money they are spending, anyway.

Your local FHA office will make all the necessary forms available to you. You should have a good supply of these on hand at all times. The forms are self-explanatory, but if you have any questions, call your HUD office for directions. The price and terms of sale will be listed in the ad showing what homes are available. FHA will not negotiate on these items. If they have listed the home as a cash out, you will have to find other means of financing the property. Usually, they will sell the property on FHA, however. You must first make an attempt to get a lender to give you a commitment on the points FHA quotes they are willing to pay. If you are not successful, FHA will secure a company for you. The closing costs on these properties are less for your buyer than would normally be expected on an FHA loan. FHA will pick up just about all closing costs, except for the insurance, taxes, and some minor closing costs.

There are several advantages to selling these homes. The competition is not as great, they are easily accessible, and by splitting the commission between the office and the selling agent and not having a listing fee, the commission will be as great as selling a home at a higher rate of commission. If the home is not sold as time goes on, FHA will usually reduce the price until you can get some good buys for your clients. Sometimes these homes are put in good repair, sometimes they aren't. Either way, FHA will advertise them "as is" and let the buyer know what work has been done. They will guarantee nothing after the transaction is closed, and normally they will not make any repairs in addition to those already made when the home was placed on the market. If you list repairs on the offer you send them, they will scratch them off and explain that all repairs have been made that they are willing to do. (Window glass might be the only exception to that. They will replace any glass broken before the final inspection, prior to closing.)

If you are having difficulty finding homes to sell, this will be a very good way to generate properties to show your FHA buyers. There is another advantage, also. With FHA, you will not have to explain what points are to your seller.

TIME-TESTED TECHNIQUES FOR FINDING FHA BUYERS

Locating and attracting FHA buyers to your office is not difficult, but does require you to use different techniques from those used to attract conventional buyers. The most effective method of building up your clientele with FHA buyers is through your advertising. The FHA buyer is generally looking for his or her first home, has a limited amount of down payment money and is looking for terms offering the lowest monthly payment possible. By emphasizing in your ads that a home can be purchased for $750 down and monthly payments of $210 including taxes and insurance, you will attract the attention of the FHA buyer.

You don't want to educate your prospects too well, but you do want them to know that you know what you are doing, and you can get almost anyone financed. Many potential buyers feel their credit prohibits them from buying a home, when in reality you can finance them through FHA. In your advertising, point out that you can finance people who have filed for bankruptcy, people with poor credit, limited income or little down payment funds.

Once every two or three weeks insert a paragraph in your line ads directed solely at the FHA and VA buyer. Thousands of people pick up the classified ads every day, dreaming of owning a home, but at the same time telling themselves they can't buy a home for a few years. They *can* buy a home now, and it's up to you to convince them that they don't have to wait—unless, of course, you want to wait five years to earn a commission.

Once you know what can be done with FHA and who can use it, you will find that buyers are everywhere. You will start working with people you never thought of as prospects before. Young people can buy FHA in most states, since the age limit has been lowered. The problem with young people at most institutions is not their age, but rather their having no credit. FHA realizes this and allows for it.

Elderly people can buy on FHA, too. FHA will not reject a loan because of concern that the buyer will not outlive the loan. The oldest buyer I know of on FHA was 81. Of course, his 63-year-old son had to cosign because of his limited income. In addition, single women have trouble borrowing conventional money for several reasons. They usually have a limited income, many lenders still discriminate against women and they don't have the resources to save up a large down payment. FHA will consider support payments, welfare assistance, social security and their wages as their income. They will look upon a single woman as just another applicant, and not as a woman in a man's world. In fact, FHA will probably be more lenient on women than on married men, because FHA has certain pressures on them.

Two people living together, whether two women, two men, or a man and a woman, can purchase a home FHA as co-mortgagors and get both their incomes counted. FHA may be the only method of financing a home for a buyer who has had past credit problems or filed for bankruptcy. When you take all the people in these categories, you have established quite a market for yourself.

Where do you find these people? Well, in addition to effective advertising, you will find them living in mobile homes, apartment complexes, working in gas stations, groceries, restaurants, offices, department stores and factories. Every time you do business with someone, even if it's just buying a cup of coffee or $2 worth of gas, hand them your card. They'll start asking you about buying a house every time. This is the one business that people always want to talk about. Open houses will usually attract the dreamers who are just looking. They really want to buy a house, but think they can't. Show them how they can. Every time someone tells me they have a problem and cannot buy a home, I tell them anyone can buy a home. I believe it, and if I can make them believe it, I have a new client.

Buyers who have already tried to buy a home FHA and failed are also good prospects. Usually the reason they weren't successful is that their agent did not know what he was doing. FHA does not keep files on the buyers, only on the property. Review the problem, correct it, find them a new home and earn yourself a commission. You may be able to use the same mortgage company or you might have to find a different one, depending upon why the loan was rejected.

The biggest help in finding FHA buyers is your attitude. If you are constantly on the lookout for an opportunity to show how much you know about FHA, the buyers will spring up from everywhere. I never tell a prospect I will try or I think I can. I tell them to pick the house, and I'll do the rest.

NINE PROFITABLE REASONS YOU SHOULD USE FHA FINANCING

FHA offers many advantages that other financing methods do not. To take advantage of a huge market that cannot qualify for other types of loans, you must be familiar with FHA. Below you will find a list of some of the reasons and ways to use FHA to increase your income and serve more customers.

1. FHA offers an interest rate that is usually lower than conventional loans.
2. FHA will insure for 30 years (35 years on some programs).
3. Almost anyone can qualify for an FHA loan, regardless of age, race, sex, or marital status.
4. You need less money down for FHA than for most methods of

financing. (Many people would never be able to purchase a
home if they needed to give a large down payment.)

5. Many homes are in a price range, location or condition that
   would cause them to be rejected by other types of financing.
6. FHA is more liberal on credit than conventional methods.
   People with credit problems, bankruptcies, etc., can purchase
   a home only with FHA financing.
7. By dealing with mortgage companies on FHA loans, you have
   an opportunity to restructure your buyer's financial status.
8. The buyers you handle will be less choosy about the home
   they buy. They know they are limited and are more interested
   in buying *a* home, rather than *the* home.
9. Any financing available to you should be used to increase your
   chances of earning a commission and selling a house.

FHA can also come in handy when selling country homes with
large pieces of ground. I once had a buyer who was interested in a
home with several acres. FHA would not give any value to ground,
other than what was necessary for a home site. We split the ground
up to be a house on an acre of land and a 10-acre piece of bare
ground. We financed the home on FHA and bought the remaining
10 acres on contract. We raised the price of the home to cover part
of the land, so the seller could realize most of his equity. As long as
it is handled properly, there is nothing wrong with this type of purchase and it solves the problem of the buyer not being able to qualify
for a large loan and the seller not wanting to tie up all his equity with
a contract.

I have often had buyers who wanted a home, but were not making enough money to qualify for an FHA loan. By selling them a
duplex or four-unit apartment building, I added income to their application so that they had enough to qualify. Income properties are
an excellent way for a young family to start out. If, after a short
period of time, they decide they do not like living in an apartment
building, you can sell them a home on FHA using the income from
the apartments to qualify them for a new home. You've earned two
commissions and provided your client with a supplementary income
and a home. There are certain guidelines that you must follow on
FHA and you need a buyer who is willing to do what is necessary in
order to get into a home.

FHA is particularly good for widows, divorced people or single
women. They will see that these people get a fair shake, if they qualify. I had a client who received social security for her two children.
She did some babysitting on the side, and I got a letter from the

social security office showing how much she received, when her next increase was due and a letter from the couple she babysat for. We were still a little short on the 35% guideline, however. FHA counted both of her incomes, both were tax-free, and she had few debts. This meant that, by not deducting taxes or payments, she was well under the 50% rule, but her income or obligations did not change for the 35% rule.

It was a rather unusual circumstance. We wrote a letter to FHA explaining that her cost of living was less than a man who had to support a wife as well as his children. We also pointed out that she was raising the children on her own and that they needed the security of owning their own home. The loan was approved without any difficulty. I have always been successful in getting FHA to deal fairly and even give more consideration to a single woman.

USING CO-MORTGAGORS TO SECURE FHA LOANS

FHA allows the buyer to obtain a co-mortgagor if his income or credit is inadequate. Depending upon the reason a co-mortgagor is needed, the main person qualifying for the loan could be the buyer or the person being used to help with the signing. For instance, if a buyer had inadequate credit, the actual person who would be under consideration would be he. If the reason a co-mortgagor is needed is job stability, insufficient income, and very bad credit, the main person under consideration would be the individual signing with him. When a co-mortgagor is involved, he must qualify just as the buyer does. It is not just a matter of signing the documents. About the only thing that is different is that he does not have to reside in the dwelling. This is where most sales people get into trouble with co-mortgagors. They fail to tell the person what will be involved.

When you are dealing with a buyer who knows that this is his only way to buy a home, getting the necessary information is not difficult; but when you have to tell a 50-year-old man that he must show the amount of money he has in the bank, a good employment record, go through a credit check, etc., he is not used to doing business that way. He has been buying things for 20 years, by just walking in and saying, "I want it," No one ever questioned him before. He is insulted. Make sure your co-mortgagors know what they are in for, or they may say, "The hell with it," before you ever get to the closing.

You can get a loan using co-mortgagors when you need additional income, such as two people buying the same property and both incomes are needed to qualify for the loan. If one of them has extensive outstanding debts or poor credit, it may hurt more than help. I have seen co-mortgagors who owed so much money that they took away from the other's borrowing power instead of adding to it. I once had a client who was the seller, his son was the buyer, and the father cosigned for the loan. This type of FHA can be useful if you know how to use it.

SIXTEEN CRITICAL POINTS TO REMEMBER WITH FHA LOANS

1. A down payment is 3% of purchase price up to $25,000. Round off the down payment to the next $50 if not exactly in $50 denominations.
2. A buyer can get his down payment as a gift, sale of an asset, or money due that will arrive before closing.
3. All closing costs can be paid by the seller. Prepaids must be paid by the buyer, however.
4. If your offer reads that the buyer is paying closing costs, the amount allotted by the appraiser for closing costs can be added onto the loan amount.
5. A buyer can already own a property and still buy FHA.
6. Anyone who qualifies on income and credit can buy FHA. Young, old, single, married, divorced, people living together, people with past credit problems, or just two people on a co-mortgage can buy.
7. FHA does not allow for pre-approval. All applications must be sent to FHA for review prior to approval.
8. Income of any type may be used, i.e. Social Security, part-time wages, babysitting, rental income, or anything else that you can get verified.
9. FHA will finance up to 30 years on existing construction and 35 years on new construction.
10. You can improve your client's application by writing letters to cover any area of weakness that exists for your buyer.
11. You can resubmit an application after a rejection. Find out why it was rejected, correct the problem and resubmit it.
12. FHA does not keep files on buyers. If you cannot get a buyer financed the first time, but feel a different mortgage company, some groundwork and a different house will get your buyer approved, sell him a different house and make a new application.

13. Writing the offer properly and preparing your seller is important. If you are doing something irregular, don't let it show up on the offer.
14. FHA will finance homes in areas that other methods might not touch.
15. You can contact your congressman and ask for his help if you feel you have not been dealt with fairly by FHA.
16. You can use FHA for non-occupant buyers, but the maximum loan is reduced to 85%.

SAMPLE LETTERS THAT WILL IMPROVE
YOUR CHANCES OF GETTING THE LOAN APPROVED

To Whom It May Concern:

I, John Doe, gave as a gift to Mr. and Mrs. Henry Doe $400 to be used as a down payment on their purchase of 518 South 13th Street. Henry is my nephew. There is no note involved nor any expectation or agreement of repayment of this money. I felt he should own his own home and therefore, I offered to give him this money.

Sincerely,

John Doe

Mr. John Doe
Indiana Mortgage Company
111 Indiana Avenue
Indianapolis, IN 46204

Dear Mr. Doe:

I was unemployed from January 25, 1975 to January 1976. During that time, I drew unemployment compensation in the amount of $85 per week.

Sincerely,

Jim Smith

Mr. John Doe
Indiana Mortgage Co.
111 Indiana Avenue
Indianapolis, IN 46204

Dear Mr. Doe:

I am writing this letter at your request to explain to you and FHA my bankruptcy, collection, and slow rating at Acme Loan Company.

In 1962, I was having difficulty with my marriage. Between loss of work and my ex-wife's spending, I saw no out but to file. The total amount filed upon was $7,500. It has been almost 14 years since the bankruptcy was discharged (November 1962), and I have none of the documents you requested. The attorney who handled my case is now deceased. Since it was so long ago, I hope it will not stop my loan from being approved.

In 1973, we did get our divorce and there was a disputed medical bill. Since I was afraid it would hurt my credit, after it was turned over to a collection agency, I paid this account.

I had a loan with Acme Loan Company at the time and with all the bills that go with a divorce, I fell behind. Once the divorce was settled, I began catching up on my payments and recently rewrote the loan to bring it up to date.

I have worked hard to be fair with my creditors even when times were rough. They, in return, have treated me fairly.

It is my hope that buying this home will make me a solid member of the community and give my family a feeling of belonging somewhere. I have chosen a home that is large enough for my family, yet well within my budget.

It is my sincere hope that you can look upon my application favorably. I would like to thank you for all the work that you have done to help me buy this home.

      Sincerely,

      Jim Smith
      100 Smith Way
      Indianapolis, IN

To Whom It May Concern:

I intend to rent the house at 4 Northwest J Street for $125 per month plus utilities. I will occupy the house as soon as it is available and will pay one month's security deposit.

Sincerely,

Jim Smith

CHAPTER THREE

An FHA or VA Loan
for Your Every Need

FHA AND VA ARE MUCH MORE THAN
LOW DOWN PAYMENT FINANCING

FHA and VA offer over thirty different methods of financing, each of which can benefit you in your efforts to secure outlets for your clients' mortgage needs. Many times, particularly in tight money markets, they are the only funds available to your buyer. These financing avenues can earn you commissions when you are working with clients who have below average incomes, need a home in an area that banks won't loan in, want investment property, require lower than normal monthly payments or when conventional money isn't available.

While most of these FHA and VA loans are available through the lenders you work with every day, few lenders will be familiar with them. Some of these thirty plus loans are available directly from FHA, Farmer's Home or VA, but, regardless of whether the government or your local lender is making the loan, you will have to be familiar with what is available to your client, how they work and what you can do to make them work for you.

FHA and VA loans can be used to finance multi-unit purchases from two to several hundred units, nursing homes, schools, businesses, farms, mobile homes, refinancing and rehabilitation or low-income housing. Chapter Three gives you the guidelines and requirements for many of these methods and suggests some ways to use them to ensure that you can finance 100% of your buyers.

FARMER'S HOME ADMINISTRATION

Farmer's Home Administration is an agency of the government, which provides financing in rural areas and unincorporated towns. They are limited to financing single-family homes that meet their requirements. The main reason they are important to you is that they will finance people unable to qualify under other methods of financing because of income. A buyer can purchase a home in a price range he would otherwise not be able to afford, and FHA will put a maturity on the loan that allows the payments to be within the borrower's means. The loan can be for up to 33 years depending on the area in which the purchaser is buying. The maximum loan attainable will also depend on the area and the home.

The homes need not have any special items, unless being built under Farmer's Home Administration to secure FHA money. If they are being erected with this idea in mind, the officer handling FHAs in the area must approve the plans, materials and construction. This officer processes the complete loan including the application, appraisal and closing. This includes used, as well as new, homes, and the officer will even do the collecting and foreclosure when necessary. Farmer's Home has two basic requirements: (1) the home must be in an unincorporated area, and (2) the buyer must be unable to obtain financing elsewhere.

The down payment and closing costs will depend upon how much money the buyer has available. If he has $200, it will be $200; if he has $300, it will be $300. The buyer has to qualify as having low income, not have too many outstanding debts and have reasonable credit. The income requirements are dependent upon the number of persons in the family and the area you are in. These requirements can be obtained from your local Farmer's Home Administration office. Your buyer should not have more than a few hundred dollars in the bank; the higher the purchase price, the more money your buyer can have.

There are a few problems with this type of loan. First, FHA practically owns the home. They have the right to inspect the proper-

ty; the owner cannot rent the property; he must notify FHA if his
income increases; and he cannot sell the home on contract or allow
his loan to be assumed. Second, most of the time the program is
short of money. This, many times, means waiting for the closing until
next month's allotment is received. If the appraisal is short, the buyer
may be permitted to pay the difference in cash, but only with FHA's
approval. Never will they allow a buyer to pay more than a few hundred dollars over the appraisal amount.

Farmer's Home Administration financing also offers loans to
those individuals who do not need extended terms or a reduced interest rate. This type of Farmer's Home Administration loan is best
used when you are in a rural area with a tight money supply or if you
have a buyer with little or no down payment money available. Your
buyer still must be unable to obtain other mortgage funds, but there
is no maximum income for him to qualify.

Farmer's Home can also be a very effective tool in financing
farms and farm equipment when used in conjunction with the Federal Land Bank or Production Credit. Used as a secondary market,
FHA can help you arrange 100% financing, including the farm ma-
chinery involved.

Farmer's Home Administration does have its negative aspects,
however. The loans take 45 to 60 days to close, FHA maintains an
unusual amount of control over the property, and the appraisal is
likely to be conservative. Even considering these negative aspects,
however, Farmer's Home is a vital and effective financing tool and
one you cannot afford to ignore.

FHA/VA COMBINATION LOANS

FHA Section 203B2 is available to veterans who have served at
least 90 days' active duty or are members of the National Guard or
Reserves. The housing requirements and income qualification are
the same as for a normal FHA loan, and this financing is available on
single-family structures only with a maximum allowable mortgage
limit of $60,000.

No down payment is required on FHA/VA loans on the first
$25,000, except the prepaids if your buyer is paying them. The buyer
must put down 5% of the amount of the purchase that exceeds
$25,000. The maximum mortgage is increased if the buyer finances
his closing costs. The only real advantage of this program is that the
veteran does not have to have 180 days of active service to qualify for
the loan.

FHA SECTION 221D2

To qualify under this program the buyers must be a family (two or more persons), related by blood or marriage or operation of law. Single persons over 62 or physically handicapped persons can also qualify. Property requirements are the same as under 203B mortgages, except that this financing is not available for homes under construction or homes that are under one year old and were not built under FHA. All homes require city inspection for code violations. The maximum mortgage will depend on the area or county in which you are selling.

The basic purpose of this program is to allow buyers to get into properties with an investment of only 3%, including closing costs. If the buyer is paying closing costs, they can be added to the mortgage and the buyer will only have his down payment to pay in cash. If the seller is paying closing costs, of course, the buyer still only has his 3% down payment.

The maximum mortgage amounts available under this program are:

Single Family – 3 bedrooms	$36,000
Single Family – 4 bedrooms	42,000
Two-Family Unit	45,000
Three-Family Unit	57,600
Four-Family Unit	68,400

The down payment required is 3% of the total acquisition costs (sales price plus closing costs plus prepaids) for single-family units, and 3% of the sales price and closing costs (prepaids must be paid in cash) on multi-units.

FHA SECTION 222 (IN SERVICE)

To qualify under this program, a veteran must have been in the service for at least two years and must at present be a member in good standing of a branch of the military. The benefit is that while the buyer is in the service, the military will pay the one-half percent insurance premium FHA charges on the loan. The property requirements are the same as Section 203B (normal FHA loan) and the maximum allowable mortgage is the same as 203B2.

The down payment requirements are 3% of the first $25,000, and 5% of anything over $25,000. The basic idea of this program was to save the veterans' VA eligibility while in the service and being moved around. Now that VA has changed its requirements to permit a veteran to use his VA as many times as he desires, within certain guidelines, this program is less useful to you, but under certain conditions, still one that can earn you a commission.

FHA 245-GRADUATED PAYMENT MORTGAGES

FHA 245 (GPM) was developed to offset the increasing problem of housing prices rising more rapidly than a buyer's income. The basic effect of GPM is that it allows your buyer to purchase 25% more home than would otherwise be possible, because his monthly payments are reduced for the first five years of the mortgage.

Since the principal obligation can never exceed the maximum insurable loan amount under a normal FHA, the buyer will normally have to make a larger down payment. The annual payments in the early years will not be enough to cover the interest, so that the loan balance will increase instead of decrease during the early period of the loan.

Five plans are available under this program:

Plan I   - Monthly mortgage payments increase 2½% for 5 years

Plan II - Monthly mortgage payments increase 5% for 5 years.

Plan III - Monthly mortgage payments increase 7½% for 5 years.

Plan IV - Monthly mortgage payments increase each year 2% for 10 years.

Plan V   - Monthly mortgage payments increase 3% for 10 years.

The maximum mortgage amount under GPM is $60,000, with a maximum term of 30 years. GPM can be used on single-family, owner-occupied homes only. Above all other considerations, FHA underwriters will need a strong assurance that the buyer has reasonable expectations of receiving a sizable increase in income over the next five years.

MAKING GRADUATED PAYMENT MORTGAGES
WORK FOR YOU

This is the most aggressive program developed by FHA since the inception of the 203B mortgage. FHA has presented you with a solution to your biggest problem: housing prices and interest rates outrunning buyers' increases in income.

To make GPM work for you, you have to concentrate on those groups of people most likely to qualify for greatly increased earnings over the next five years. These groups include young attorneys, doctors, college graduates, CPAs, middle management employees, coaches, or anyone else who can get verification of their income increasing substantially in the future.

This market is particularly lucrative for you, because these are the very individuals who feel a need to own a home that lives up to their image or is comparable to the homes of the people they work and socialize with. Now you have a means to help them solve their problems, and earn a commission check for yourself.

FHA SECTION 235

This program is for low-income buyers who are purchasing newly constructed or rehabilitated housing. Substantial rehabilitation requires a minimum of 25% of repairs or improvements to be a part of the home's value. Any homes constructed under this program must be built within FHA restrictions. The down payment requirements under FHA 235 are set forth below.

Down payment must be equal to the greater of:

a. 3% of the first $25,000 plus 10% of the balance over $25,000
b. 6% of the FHA estimate of cost of acquisition. The cost of investment may include closing costs and prepaid expenses.

This is a low income program, so the income and maximum mortgage amount will vary from area to area. You can get the maximum income allowable from a mortgage company in your area, but basically you can figure the buyer should be making less than the average for your area. The number of persons in the family will determine how many bedrooms the home must have, the price allowable for mortgage and income required to qualify. FHA 235, however, is becoming less and less valuable to brokers as FHA becomes more strict with the individuals. There has been so much publicity about the number of times this program has been deceived, that FHA has become reluctant to approve buyers who do not meet their requirements perfectly.

FHA MULTI-UNIT FINANCING

FHA offers multi-unit financing under several programs that do not require the owner to occupy the premises. Most of these programs are designed for large apartment developments, while others are for single-unit condominium financing. FHA is very active in the financing of multi-unit apartments, nursing homes, shopping centers, mobile home parks and even colleges. In this chapter we will discuss some of the more useful programs for real estate salespeople.

FHA 234(C) – CONDOMINIUM UNIT FINANCING

FHA will insure the financing for the purchase of individual units in condominium projects containing four or more units. If the project has more than eleven units, however, the project mortgage must be, or at one time must have been, insured under some section of FHA other than 213 (Sales or Management Cooperative).

It is important to note here that a condominium need contain only four units. This leaves the possibility that a creative real estate salesperson could convert a four-unit or larger apartment building to a condominium with individual unit owners to move a building and end up with four sales instead of just one.

All terms of the mortgage are in line with a normal FHA loan (203B), and the processing shouldn't require any special attention on your part, other than what you would normally do to get an FHA loan approved.

FHA 221(D)(3) – LOW AND MODERATE INCOME HOUSING PROJECTS

The purpose of this loan is to finance construction or even rehabilitation of a rental or cooperative apartment complex for low and moderate income families, elderly persons or handicapped individuals. Up to 10% of the units may be occupied by low or moderate income single persons under 62 years of age, and priority must be given in occupancy to individuals displaced by urban renewal or other government action.

The insurable limits per unit depend upon the type and size of unit, with a range from $11,240 to $32,000. The maximum term of the mortgage is 40 years with 90% financing available.

TITLE X MORTGAGE INSURANCE FOR LAND DEVELOPMENT

Under this program FHA will finance the purchase of land and the development of building sites for subdivisions or new communities, including water, and sewer systems, streets, etc. FHA will insure 80% of the estimated value of the land before development plus 90% of the estimated cost of development or 85% of the estimated value upon completion, whichever is less. While the term of the mortgage is only 10 years, a longer term is provided for new water and sewer systems.

FHA 207 – MORTGAGE INSURANCE FOR MOBILE HOME COURTS

The purpose of this mortgage is to finance the construction or rehabilitation of mobile home courts. While the maximum mortgage amount is $3,250 per space, the per-mortgage and per-space limits may be increased up to 45% if the cost levels in the area require more than the allowed amount.

FHA will insure 90% of the cost with terms from 20 to 40 years maximum, depending upon the mortgage amount and the growth pattern of the area.

FHA 232 – NURSING HOMES FINANCING

FHA will insure a mortgage for the construction or rehabilitation of nursing homes or intermediate care facilities accommodating 20 or more patients. Major items of equipment may be included in the mortgage.

The loan value ratio for such a facility is 90% with a mortgage term of 40 years.

MAKING APPLICATION AND PROCESSING MULTI-UNIT AND NURSING HOMES MORTGAGES

FHA will insure for 90% of the replacement cost and will grant a maturity of up to 40 years. Your first step is to meet with the Chief of Mortgage Credit at your local FHA office. You should have information pertaining to the site location, need for such a facility and the capability of the applicant to handle such an undertaking. If FHA sees any potential in the proposal, they will invite an application for a feasibility analysis. If, after the study has been made, FHA still feels it is a workable proposal, they will ask for an application for a mortgage commitment. When advised by FHA to apply for an insured mortgage, sponsors should obtain the application form from an approved lender.

The limits per unit are adjusted by FHA from time to time, so the limits applying to your area at the time you begin the application should be requested from FHA. The fee for processing your application will be $3 per thousand dollars of the amount applied for. This fee is broken down into three parts: one-third is due when you submit an application for a feasibility study, one-third is due when you submit the application, and one-third is due when you file for the commitment.

These programs are available to individuals, partnerships, corporations, and private nonprofit groups. The main requirements are that the borrower be on solid ground financially, have experience in the area being undertaken and that there is a need for the proposed project. You must show FHA that the debt service can be carried by the income from the project. FHA will guide you step by step through the processing, but you must make sure that not only is the applicant qualified, but also that the general contractor and architect are accomplished in their fields.

FHA MOBILE HOME LOANS – TITLE I, SECTION 2

FHA will insure the financing for the purchase of a mobile home which will be the buyer's principal residence. As housing costs rise, more and more families are purchasing mobile homes. If you as a real estate salesperson are to get your share of this market, you must be able to provide buyers with financing just as readily as a mobile home sales lot does.

The mobile home must meet all HUD standards. The maximum loan, excluding finance charges, is $10,000 on single-wides with a 12-year maturity and $15,000 on double-wides with a 15-year maturity.

DOZENS OF FHA PROGRAMS FOR DOZENS OF FINANCING NEEDS

FHA has for too long been neglected for other than single-family, owner-occupied financing. In periods of tight money, FHA can help you solve almost any problem you encounter. If you have a financing problem or need, the chances are excellent that FHA has a program that will work for you. An afternoon spent at your regional FHA office can enlighten you on the dozens of financing programs available to you and your clients.

CHAPTER FOUR

VA Financing: An Untapped Market

VA financing is one of the most flexible, useful and exciting tools available to the real estate agent. It can also be one of the most profitable tools. Why? Because VA financing is the only *single* mortgage source that allows the buyer to purchase a home without investing any money, since no down payment is required, and the seller can pay all of the buyer's closing costs—even his prepaids. Now, when you start talking about people who don't have any money, your list of clients is lengthened considerably, isn't it?

FIVE PROFITABLE REASONS TO USE VA FINANCING

Besides providing your buyers with a means of purchasing a home without requiring funds for a down payment or closing costs, VA offers five other advantages over conventional financing.

While the Veterans' Administration does not loan your client the mortgage funds, they do guarantee the loan, which means that if they approve the loan, the lender approves the loan. Mortgage companies, in particular, will then work to help you get the loan approved.

Lenient Guidelines

First , VA will be more liberal than anyone else when considering your buyer's qualifications. They feel an obligation to the men and women who have served to protect our country and will do anything within reason to see that the veteran gets the home of his choice. VA will listen to the veteran's explanations of problems, consider every avenue of income and reconsider an application upon appeal when new information is presented.

Higher Appraisals

The chances of a higher appraisal are much greater with VA than with conventional financing. The appraiser will take the going point quote into consideration when appraising a property, as well as the local market trends. By providing the appraiser with comparables, accompanying him during the inspection and advising him of the appraisal you need, you can almost guarantee that you will get an appraisal that will please both buyer and seller.

Lower Interest Rates

Mortgages financed with a VA guarantee offer the lowest interest rates available. VA mortgages are also written for the maximum maturity. The combination of these two factors gives you lower payments, permitting your buyer to qualify for a loan with less income or to purchase a more expensive home than he otherwise would be able to afford.

No Redlining

While redlining (lenders' practice of not loaning in certain areas) is illegal, it is not uncommon. Most conventional lenders have certain areas in each community for which they will not make loans. VA does not redline, which gives you an outlet for loans in these areas and provides you with possibly your only means of moving this type of property; nor does VA have minimum or maximum loan limits, allowing you to sell lower-priced property when the opportunity arises.

Open Line of Communication

VA has a better line of communication directly with the buyer, lender or agent than any other financing outlet. They are always willing to discuss how they reviewed a loan, what factors caused the application to be rejected and what might be done to get the decision reversed.

Housing Requirements for VA Financing

Of course, the home must meet VA's minimum property standards. Most homes fit one of two categories—those that are of new construction and VA has approved their specifications prior to their being built, or those that are over one year old. If the property does not meet either of these standards, VA will require additional information, which consists of:

1. All permits issued by local authorities.
2. At least three copies of specifications, plot plans and Description of Materials. (Forms are available from the mortgage company.)
3. A statement from the builder that the house was built in accordance with local building codes, that he is a small builder and has not built under VA jurisdiction before, and that he will bear the cost of a compliance inspection (usually $12.50). Also, the builder must sign a Description of Materials.
4. The veteran must sign a statement saying he is aware the property was not built under VA jurisdiction and that he will not hold VA responsible for any defects in the future, and that he has seen the specifications, if indeed he has. He too, must sign a Description of Materials.

If you know in advance what needs to be done on homes of under one year and you get all your data together, it will not be a difficult loan to process.

MINIMUM PROPERTY STANDARDS FOR VA

Below is a list of points for you to watch on VA appraisals. These are by no means all the points considered by the appraiser, but rather the major areas that you should be concerned with when considering a home for VA financing.

FURNACE-VA will accept space heaters or wall furnaces with no requirements on heating ducts in each room as long as the unit is adequate for the home.

ROOF, GUTTERS, AND EAVES-Roof should be in good condition. VA always requires gutters and downspouts. Eaves must be in good repair.

PAINT, PLASTER, AND WALLPAPER-Paint on house, garage and outbuildings should not be chipped or peeling. Tuck pointing might be required if the outside plaster is in bad condition. Interior condition need not be clean (appraises better if it is); however, plaster, paper, paneling or drywall should not be in need of repair.

STEPS, HANDRAILINGS-These must always be in good repair. Handrailings are always required; especially watch basement steps and railings.

AGE-VA has no maximum age for the dwelling, but VA may reduce the number of years on the loan if the appraiser feels the condition of the house is not such to expect the economic life to outlast the 30 years normally granted.

GARAGE-VA will require the garage to have good paint, roof, windows and be structurally sound. If the garage is in disrepair, it would be better to advise the appraiser that the garage will be torn down.

WIRING-VA does *not* require 100-amp wiring. No wiring should be exposed.

PLUMBING-Of course, the plumbing should be in good working order. If you are financing a multi-unit, each unit must have kitchen and bathroom facilities. For instance, if you were selling a four-unit with two of the units being sleeping rooms, the application would have to show two units, with the two sleeping rooms being added to the apartments. Of course, the building would have to have the physical characteristics to make this temporary change feasible.

WINDOWS AND DOORS-Windows should not be cracked and doors cannot have large holes in them. Generally, all closets or openings must have doors or curtains.

SEPTIC AND WELL-VA will always require a Health Department approval of well and septic tank.

TERMITES-VA always requires a termite inspection.

BUILDING AND ZONING COMPLIANCE-On older homes and apartment buildings, VA will sometimes require a letter from the Bureau of Building Codes, stating that the property meets all minimum requirements of local zoning and building codes. This certification can be obtained from city hall and has never presented me any difficulty.

VA is more liberal on the house than FHA. This allows you to sell the lower-priced or older home with less difficulty. The appraisal fee is $60 plus $10 for each additional unit. For instance, a three-unit apartment building would cost $80. The maximum number of units that can be financed VA is four, unless more than one veteran is involved in the purchase.

SUCCESSFUL TECHNIQUES FOR GETTING A HIGH APPRAISAL

It is beneficial for you to go with the appraiser for the inspection of the property. You will get an opportunity to see his reaction, remind him of the appraisal requested, and see that he doesn't get any surprises, such as violent dogs, disgruntled tenants, talkative owners or a locked door. Help him measure. Answer his questions. In other words, make his job as easy as possible.

In most areas the appraiser will be local and inspect on contract, rather than as an employee of VA. If this is true in your area, you have a rare opportunity to affect the outcome of an appraisal. Most appraisers want to give you the requested amount, but many times they just don't see the value in the property. You can better your chances of getting a full appraisal by proving the value is there. Give the appraiser a list of three comparables that make your property look good. If he can back up his appraisal with good comparables for support, he won't hesitate to turn in the amount you requested. He will also enjoy appraising for you if you do part of his legwork by getting the comparables. (Remember, you can appeal the appraisal if you are not satisfied with the outcome. All that is necessary is for you to submit proof of why you feel the appraisal should be raised.)

PREPARING THE SELLER FOR VA FINANCING

You will cut down on time, frustration and upset sellers if you evaluate the house at the time you acquire the listing. If the house you are giving your presentation on falls into a situation that calls for VA financing, tell the owner at that time. Explain why you feel it is necessary that he consider VA as a possibility for financing the sale of his home. The reason may be the price range the home falls into, the area will not attract conventional buyers, or the size of the home might suggest a family just starting in their first home. Explain in dollars what this means to him, as well as what points are, what is involved in the way of closing costs, what repairs he can anticipate and how long it will take to finance the property. This allows you several options. He will accept the idea, consider it or refuse it. Either way, he will at least be familiar with VA when you bring him an offer.

This technique will also give you an opportunity to build the points into the listing price, which will remove one of the biggest stumbling blocks to smooth VA transactions. You might even suggest that a VA appraisal be obtained prior to an offer being made, so the seller will have a good idea of where he stands and you can advertise the property with VA terms. There is a good reason to secure a VA appraisal if the choice is between VA and FHA. VA will not accept FHA's appraisal, but FHA will, in most cases, accept VA's appraisal. This means that by having a VA appraisal, you are covered for either FHA or VA financing.

COMPLETING THE APPRAISAL REQUEST

The appraisal request will be issued by the lender and is basically self-explanatory. There are only a couple of points that require special attention. First, do not list drapes, appliances not built-in, or rugs not tacked down on the appraisal. These items will take away from the value of the property rather than add to it. Second, note on the appraisal that your office should be contacted for a key. This will give you an opportunity to accompany the appraiser on his inspection.

QUALIFYING THE BUYER FOR 100% FINANCING

We will start by deciding who is eligible and to what point. If the veteran served in any part of active service from September 16, 1940 to July 25, 1947, from June 27, 1950 to January 31, 1955, or if he had a service-connected disability from a period of active duty, he must have served 90 days or more of active duty to be eligible for VA benefits. After January 31, 1955, the veteran must have served 181 days of continuous service or, in the case of service-connected disability, 90 days is sufficient. All of the above requirements include an essential item—the active duty must have been under conditions other than dishonorable. A dishonorable discharge does not automatically disqualify a veteran, however. He can request a review of his case before a three-member panel and ask that he be granted benefits. If he served his total service time from July 25, 1947 to June 27, 1950, the veteran is not eligible for a VA loan. If he is currently in the service, the veteran must have served 181 days of continuous active duty or more. National Guard time will not accrue for VA benefits. Widows and widowers of veterans who died as a result of a service injury or illness can also qualify for their spouses' benefits.

COMPUTING YOUR BUYER'S ENTITLEMENT

Veterans who have not purchased property using their VA entitlement to date will be issued a $25,000 eligibility. All veterans desiring to use partial entitlement will need their previously issued certificate of eligibility so as to determine their remaining amount. Veterans may use their VA entitlement as many times as they wish, with the following requirements:

1. If previous loan has been paid off, veteran has full $25,000 entitlement
2. If veteran has previously used part of his eligibility, he can use the remainder up to $25,000

Example: VA guarantees 60% of the loan or $25,000, whichever is less. If the veteran bought a house VA for $20,000 in 1971, he used $12,000 of his eligibility. The mortgage company will loan four times the amount of remaining eligibility. This means your buyer could purchase a $52,000 house with no money down. (Some people seem to think that a $25,000 eligibility means a veteran can only buy a home for that amount or that a veteran needs a down payment to purchase a house.)

When using partial entitlement, veterans may also put down cash that a mortgage company will loan four to one on. Let's take the same $13,000 eligibility, for instance. The veteran can put down $1,000 and increase his loan to $56,000. VA does not set a limit on the maximum loan that can be secured with VA financing. Mortgage companies will usually only go four times the remaining eligibility, but other institutions will go higher than that at times.

UTILIZING A VETERAN'S ENTITLEMENT TO YOUR ADVANTAGE

A veteran does not have to sell his present home before buying VA again. He must intend to live in the new home, but he can have more than one VA loan at a time. I have used VA to sell a veteran an investment property, and then, as soon as he is ready to move, sell him a home using his remaining entitlement. A point to remember here is that tens of thousands of veterans purchased a home many years ago when their entitlement was less. A veteran buying a home as late as 1967 had only $7,500 eligibility. He may have purchased a $30,000 home and still have $17,500 eligibility remaining. Every veteran's eligibility has increased, even if he used it up when it was less.

Getting the information to the veterans who think they are no longer entitled is the most important step. Some veterans have no idea of what their eligibility means to them. Many veterans think their entitlement ran out, since they were in the service many years ago and never used it. All veteran's rights on real estate loans have been extended and there is a big market for those agents who know how to use VA. Ask everyone you talk to if they meet any of the VA qualifications.

When using partial entitlement, it is wise to first obtain the veteran's previously used certificate of eligibility, along with copies of DD 214's issued to him. Apply through any mortgage company to obtain allowable entitlement. You should also be aware that a veteran can have his liability released from a loan, if that loan is assumed by a veteran willing to use his eligibility to replace the original borrower's liability. This is just like selling the home VA, except that an appraisal is not required. Unless your seller insists, it is better to stay away from this type of assumption. If a mortgage company holds the loan on a house, there is no easier assumption. They do not require a credit report, there is no time delay, and no approval from the mortgage company is necessary in most cases. Even allowing for mail time, the transaction can be closed in a week. On the other hand, if you are required to submit your new buyer to VA in order to get the seller's liability released, you will be faced with almost six weeks waiting time.

QUALIFYING YOUR BUYER'S INCOME

When qualifying a buyer's income for a VA loan, you must have a minimum amount left after all deductions are made. This amount depends on the price range of the home and the number of members in the family. Following you will find the VA Budget Allowance Chart. After following the qualifying instructions and work sheet, you can use this Chart as a guide to see if your buyer has enough money left monthly to qualify.

VA Budget Allowance	
Mortgage up to $15,000	$375
Mortgage of $15,000 to $20,000	$410
Mortgage of $20,000 to $25,000	$440
Mortgage of $25,000 to $30,000	$520
Mortgage of $30,000 to $35,000	$612
Mortgage of over $35,000	1% of each $1,000 over $35,000

This Chart is for a family of four or less. For each member over four, add 10% to the minimum balance. VA will adjust these amounts from time to time, if they feel inflation has caused the cost of living to increase beyond these figures. Your mortgage company should keep you up-to-date on any adjustments made by VA.

Qualifying Instructions

1. Compute one month's principal, interest, taxes and insurance, for proposed housing expense.
2. Compute estimated maintenance and utilities.
3. Compute Social Security (6.76 times gross monthly income / 8.10 times gross monthly income if self-employed).
4. Compute state and local taxes. (Charts are available from most mortgage companies.)
5. Compute federal withholding tax. (Charts are available from most mortgage companies).
6. Compute total monthly debts exceeding 5 months in duration including alimony and child support.
7. Place totals of lines 1 through 6 in block 7.
8. Compute gross monthly income.
9. Refer to VA Budget Allowance Chart. Place appropriate figure pertaining to mortgage amount on line.
10. Subtract line 9 from gross monthly income on line 8.
11. Block 10 must exceed Block 7.

WORK SHEET

1. Principal and interest.. _____
2. Maintenance and Utilities................................ _____
3. Social Security.. _____
4. State and Local Taxes...................................... _____
5. Federal Withholding Taxes............................... _____
6. Recurring Debts.. _____
7. Total.. [_____]
8. Gross Monthly Income..................................... _____
9. Budget Allowance.. _____
10. Income Figure for Comparison......................... [_____]

GETTING ALL OF YOUR CLIENT'S INCOME COUNTED

Income that may be used in consideration for a VA loan includes, but is not limited to, the veteran's full-time wages, part-time wages, overtime, spouse's income, pension, disability, Social Security, rents, trust funds, property sold on contract, commissions, bonuses and self-employment income. A forthcoming raise may be used to push your buyer over the line, if his employer will verify the raise and the date it is to take effect. If your buyer is self-employed, you will have to show past tax returns, as well as profit and loss statements for two years, and asset and liability sheets, and have each of them certified by your client's accountant.

If your buyer has recently changed jobs, you can still get all his income counted, if you can show that he was employed in a related field previously, and that his new position is secure from probable layoff. The employment verification is extremely important to your cause. A strong verification will make up for weaknesses in other parts of his application. I have found it useful to call the Personnel Manager if I am acquainted with him, or have the buyer contact his Personnel Department and explain what is needed on the verification. They are usually glad to help if they know what you need. If your veteran has been on a job for only a short time, a letter from his previous employer will help. If you need to get overtime or bonuses included for consideration by VA, you must get the income verified by the employer as being of a steady nature. You may need to turn in your buyer's past W-2s to prove this income has been reliable in the past. You can also improve your client's application by having the employment verification show that he is a valued employee and thought of highly by his company.

If you are running over or close on the income-to-debt ratio, you can eliminate certain obligations by paying them down to less than five months or by consolidating loans to reduce the monthly debt. Credit Unions do not usually show up on a credit report. If you do not wish a Credit Union debt to show, don't turn in any deposit the buyer has in his savings. When the mortgage company sends out the verification of deposit, they will also inquire about any outstanding loan the buyer has with the Credit Union. You are often better off without the deposit. Later in this chapter you will find letters that may be used to enhance a buyer's income picture.

STRENGTHENING YOUR BUYER'S CREDIT PICTURE

Although a purchaser's credit must be up-to-date when VA receives the buyer's application and cannot show any outstanding collections, past collections or slow credit ratings will not disqualify your buyer in themselves. This is one of the aspects of VA financing that makes it so attractive. VA will be more liberal on their credit requirements than any other source of financing. If your buyer does have or has had credit problems, it is best that you find out prior to the loan application so you can take the necessary steps to correct the problem. If he has an outstanding collection, get it paid. If he is in arrears on his monthly obligations, bring them up-to-date. Write the letters you need to explain the collection or slowness of payment. (Sample letters are included at the end of this chapter.) Turn them in with the application. This will save you a lot of time as well as let the mortgage company know what they will have to do going in. Your letters should always be addressed to the mortgage officer handling the loan, and be from the buyer's point of view. They should be signed by the buyer, unless they are from another source or reference. Make them logical, full of "hard times and a few tears." A divorce, illness, past layoff (not recent), or disagreement over an obligation, are all good reasons for collections or lateness of payment. The letters must show sincerity, logic, a solution to the problem (it's important that whatever the reason for the past situation, it has been solved and everything is now steady) and a need to own a home in order to make the buyer feel more a part of the community and make his family more secure.

CHANGING POOR CREDIT INTO A CLOSED SALE

An old friend came to me one day and wanted to buy a home VA. He made good money, had years of seniority, and felt his credit was in good condition. We found a suitable home and made application for a loan. When the credit report came back, I knew we were in trouble. If he had told me the truth at the start, we could have corrected the problems before submitting the application. His credit was rated slow, three loans were in arrears and he had an outstanding collection. To make things worse, the collection was on a loan he had cosigned for someone else. The party was not willing to pay the collection because he disagreed with the bill. My client was not willing to pay it because he did not make the debt. After some convincing, the friend agreed to pay the collection. I then went to one of the loan companies he owed and arranged a consolidation loan for two of the loans on which he was behind. The loan company even agreed to give me a letter stating the purpose of the loan, and that they felt my client was a good credit risk. The last loan company I spoke to agreed not to label him slow on the new credit report if he brought his account up to date immediately. We then wrote a letter stating that the reason for his recent slowness of payment was because of his daughter's illness. It was not covered by insurance, and he lost several days of work going back to the doctor. We wrote a letter explaining the collection and got a letter of reference from his landlord. We also pointed out his past credit and his need for the home. It was closer to work and he and his family would feel more secure and a part of the community. VA granted the loan and my buyer had become a home owner through what was probably the only method he could ever use to buy a home.

ELIMINATING BANKRUPTCIES AS AUTOMATIC REJECTIONS

Many people, including the buyers, think that a past bankruptcy cancels the buyer's chances of getting a loan. This is not true. VA will approve the buyer with past bankruptcies of over one and one-half years old. What is necessary is for the buyer to show VA a logical reason for the bankruptcy, a good credit rating since, and an honest desire on the part of the buyer to mend his "misguided" ways. This can be accomplished by supplying VA with the following information:

1. A copy of the bankruptcy discharge papers.

2. A copy of the list of creditors and a statement showing which creditors were repaid.
3. Letters showing good credit since bankruptcy. These can come from places where he has had an account, individuals who have loaned him money, stores that he has had lay-aways with, gas stations, or the credit union at work.
4. The smaller the bankruptcy and the more creditors repaid, the better the bankruptcy looks.
5. A letter stating the reason for the bankruptcy. A business failure, divorce, doctor bills that could not be paid, garnishments with threat of loss of job, demanding creditors when payment in full was not possible, an attorney's advice, or a major dispute over a claim, are all good reasons for filing bankruptcy.
6. A letter showing that the veteran has learned his lesson, wishes to have another chance and the benefit his family will receive if the loan is approved.

I have financed veterans with all types of bankruptcies, anywhere from 18 months to 14 years prior to application. This may be the only means for most of them to buy a home. If you have doubts after your letters are written, having your buyer put down $500 or $1,000 will swing a lot of weight with VA. It shows that he is putting something of himself into the house. Never let a bankruptcy scare you away from a buyer. If you can show him how to buy a home, he will jump at the opportunity. He knows he would be lucky to ever own a home again and he will not let an opportunity pass him by. It is important when dealing with this type of buyer that you don't sell him too much house. VA will not want to see him get in over his head again.

I WANT TO BUY ON CONTRACT

One of my salespeople was having difficulty selling a new prospect. The buyer only wanted to look at property he could purchase on contract. She was not having much luck and came to me with the problem. Her client had nine years on the job, had an excellent income and was a veteran, but she could not get him to talk anything except contract. He had purchased a property on contract previously and was pleased with that method of buying a home. I realized that he probably had a credit problem he did not want us to know about. The saleslady was sure this could not be it, because of his good job and the nice car that he drove. Reluctantly, she agreed to run a credit check, but felt sure it would be good. It was terrible. He had filed for bankruptcy several years before, had an outstanding collection, and had not reestablished his credit since the bankruptcy. I asked her to have him come in and meet with us. I told him that, as was standard procedure, we had run a credit check on him and discovered the bankruptcy. I explained to him that although we were having difficulty finding him a seller willing to sell on contract in a location he desired, we did have several properties available on VA and that I felt he had a good chance of qualifying for a VA loan. He was hesitant at first, but I told him we could get the job done and it would greatly increase his borrowing power in the community.

He was a changed man. In two days we had found him a suitable home and we started to work. The collection was paid off and a letter was written explaining that the collection was a result of a bill his former wife made and that he was unaware it had been filed. We got a copy of the discharge papers, a copy of his divorce decree, a copy of the list of creditors and a letter explaining why he filed for bankruptcy. At the time he filed, he had been cut to a three-day week, and his creditors were not willing to accept partial payments, so they garnisheed his wages. In those days, you were discharged if you did not get a garnishment cleared up within thirty days, and until the matter was cleared up, you were laid off. He needed his job, so he filed for bankruptcy to get rid of the garnishment. In his letter we pointed out that this was an example of why the law concerning garnishments and employers needed to be changed and that he was just sorry it didn't happen in time to save him.

We got letters from people he had borrowed money from. We even got a letter from where he bought his car, even though he paid cash for it. The letter stated that he had purchased the auto and paid for it as agreed. He did. They agreed on cash. We got a strong letter from the contract seller for the property he already owned. The loan was approved on the first application and we sold a home to a man who thought he could never get a house financed again.

VA, as stated earlier, is more liberal than any other type of financing. The reason is simple. VA feels an obligation to the veteran for service rendered to his country. They are there to help these people. If there is any way for them to approve the loan, they will. I have made many trips to VA when my buyer was in trouble. A personal call or visit by the veteran is also beneficial. He can answer their questions, explain why he would like to have the loan and if he has a good personality, he will greatly improve his chances.

HELPING VA TO MAKE THE RIGHT DECISION

I never argue with VA. I only try to assist the buyer by explaining his cause. I don't push if I'm not right. If you are wrong and argue, VA may wonder if you are right at times when you are. It is helpful to get to know the people at VA. Even if your contact is not with the loan processing department, he can tell you whom to talk to, what points to make and put in a good word for you. We once even called the director of the Veteran's Administration in Washington, D.C. We knew him from political meetings, so we could at least get him on the phone. The local VA had twice turned down our buyer because they felt his income was not adequate. They would not count his annual bonus, nor the rental income from the property he was buying. We picked up the phone and explained our dilemma. We received a call from the local VA within the hour saying they had reviewed the case and were going to grant the loan.

A call from your buyer to his senator or congressman can also produce fast and positive results. Knowing whom to talk to and how to get them to see the application from your point of view will often make the difference. The VA will listen to your case moreso than will any other lending facility. They honestly want to make the loan if they can feel it is the right thing to do. Respect them and they will, in return, be fair with you.

REVERSING A DECISION TO REJECT THE BUYER
AND/OR PROPERTY

A local businessman came to us and expressed an interest in buying a new building for his store. He had no money to work with, since it was all tied up in inventory. He was a veteran, however, and wanted to use his VA if possible. We started looking for a building that met his unusual requirements. It had to be in a good business location, have a nice storeroom, yet have living quarters to qualify for VA. We located such a place and went to work.

Our first concern was the building. It was actually a five-unit apartment building with a handsome storeroom downstairs. We had to reduce this to a four-unit building for the appraisal, which was simply a matter of completing the appraisal request properly.

Once this was done, we started on our buyer's income. He had worked for a competitor until a little over a year ago. This did not give us much to work on. We gathered the necessary P & L statements, asset and liability sheets and letters showing the relationship between his present business and his past experience.

When we received the appraisal, we had been cut $3,000. The appraiser felt that this was more a commercial property than a residential one. We appealed the appraisal and sent in our comparables, along with a letter explaining that this property was to be used primarily as a residence.

We got the higher appraisal, but were turned down because of the weak income figures the buyer had to show. I grabbed our files and the buyer and made a trip to VA. I pointed out that the buyer would have the income from the apartments, would be saving money, since he was now renting a house and a storeroom, and that he had a good record in the business. The buyer showed new income figures for the newest quarter and reminded them of his good credit record. The official agreed to grant the loan, if we could provide certified profit and loss statements showing the figures we had given him. We did this and the loan was granted.

This points up the importance of taking the buyer with you. VA has an opportunity to meet a person, not just see an application. To them, you are just after a commission. *You* can't be too pushy, but the buyer can.

WRITING AN OFFER WITH VA FINANCING THAT WILL SATISFY BUYER, SELLER, LENDER, AND VA

It is important that your offer to purchase be written correctly. It should state the amount of loan required, the type of financing, the number of years requested on the loan, the interest rate anticipated, the monthly payment and who is to pay what closing costs. It should show enough earnest money to cover all the buyer's closing costs, if indeed he is paying any of his own closing costs. Do not include on your offer (the copy that goes to VA) such items as drapes, curtains, rugs, or appliances. VA will sometimes deduct the value of these items from the appraisal.

VA requires original signatures from the buyer and seller on the copy of the offer they receive. Never turn in an offer that shows a counter-offer. It usually turns out that if VA discovers a counter-offer, the commitment will be for the first amount. The offer should always be neat, complete, and match all information given on the application. Do not show repairs that are to be made on the VA copy of the offer to purchase. Your copy, as well as the copy you furnish the buyer and seller, will show these repairs. If the seller has agreed to make the repairs, it is best to get them done before the appraisal is made. If VA becomes aware of repairs that have been agreed to, they might require a certain method of making them that would slow down the closing or they might even lower the appraisal. Don't show earnest money as a note on VA's copy since that would be worse than not having any earnest money. Put yourself in the place of a VA reviewer and make sure the proposition makes sense, matching all other information turned in to VA.

PRESENTING YOUR OFFER TO THE SELLERS

As you already know, all the advertising, showings and the offer to purchase are worth nothing if you don't get the offer accepted. Now that you have sold the buyer, you have to sell the seller. If the groundwork has been laid properly, it will not be difficult to get the VA offer accepted. Many times, however, this cannot be done. It might be a property that you did not anticipate going VA, or perhaps the listing agent was unfamiliar with VA and didn't suggest it to the seller.

The first step I take in solving the problem is to prepare the buyer. I explain what the seller is going to have to pay in order for the buyer to get a loan. These costs are the buyer's negotiating factor. Therefore, his offer should be for the full listed price. This gives you a point in your favor when you present the offer. Next, I list the closing items and their cost. (You will find these at the end of this segment.) I deduct these from the amount of the offer to reach the seller's net figure. I make the appointment to present the offer to the seller, after obtaining an oral credit report on my buyer.

Presenting a VA offer is only slightly different from presenting any other type of offer. Point out the little things that you know will not create much resistance, then hand the offer to the seller to read, telling him that, although it is a full-priced offer, he has closing costs involved. After he has read over the offer, tell him you ran a credit check on the buyer and what it showed (briefly), and that you feel he is a good buyer. At this point, pull out your figures on his points and closing costs. Here is where most salespeople fall into a trap. They dwell on the closing costs, arguing the necessity of each. The seller gets so upset over the principle of paying these costs that you never get him back to what really matters—his net figure. You should briefly run down the list, explaining only the items that he questions and then only with the simple explanation that they are normal closing costs incurred when dealing with mortgage companies. Explain points as simply as possible. This will not be too difficult if you understand the reasons points are necessary. If you make your explanation too involved, the seller will get totally confused. Simply explain that points are necessary to make the rate of return to the purchaser of the loan attractive, compared to other investments. Whether they are good or bad, they are necessary in order to sell the house. You must get the seller to consider them as a reduction of the sales price. Your job is not to get the seller to agree with points or the reason for them. All you want is for him to agree to the net figure he will receive. Convince your seller that these costs are no more than a bargaining factor for the buyer. It is the same as accepting a lower offer on his home.

It is also wise to inform your seller how long he can expect to wait for the closing and what repairs you feel will be necessary. If you have trouble getting your seller to agree, point out the reasons I gave you earlier for his home needing to be sold VA. You will get less resistance from a seller who has been waiting for an offer for a couple of months, since after seeing the lack of response to his property, he won't be too hard to convince. You should always leave a copy of the estimated costs with your seller and retain a copy for yourself to eliminate any misunderstanding that might occur.

CLOSING COSTS NEED NOT BE A PROBLEM

Below is a list of closing costs involving a normal VA loan with a mortgage company. If you are dealing with a bank or savings and loan, you may not have the title and survey costs or prepaids. The amount of these costs will vary from area to area. Any of these costs may be paid by either party. Don't forget discount points and the seller's normal costs that are not included in this list.

Origination Fee	1% of the loan
Appraisal	$60.00
Credit Report	$15.00
Title Insurance	$75.00 up to $30,000, then $2.50 per $1,000 thereafter
Title Examination	$50.00
Judgment Search	$15.00
Closing Fee	$100.00
Recording Fees	$12.50
Termite Inspection	$15.00

Survey	$100.00
Photos	$15.00
Deeds	$15.00 to $25.00
Prepaids	

Two Months' Taxes
First Year and Two Months' Insurance
Interest From Date of Closing Until
End of Month

You should tell the seller that certain inspections might be required by licensed contractors and that a reinspection may be necessary by VA, if there are any repairs required. These inspections will cost approximately $15.00 each. It is better to overestimate the cost than to have a seller come up short at the closing. After the closing is scheduled, and the closing agent has a draft of the closing statements, get a copy and call the buyer and seller. Review the net figure with the seller and double-check the amount the buyer is to pay. By doing this a day or two ahead of time, you have a chance to solve any problems that arise before arriving at the closing.

DIRECT LOANS FROM VA

There are certain areas in this country where the lending institutions will not make VA loans. The Veteran's Administration makes available direct loans if these areas meet certain qualifications. The veteran must still be able to qualify with his income and credit as he would if dealing with a mortgage company. The basic intention of the VA Direct Loan program is to supply home financing to eligible veterans in areas where private financing is not available. Eligible areas are designated by VA as housing credit shortage areas. You know whether VA money is available in your area or not. If not, contact your nearest VA office to see if your area qualifies for VA direct loans.

Direct loans can be obtained for the same purposes as regular VA loans, with the exception of apartment buildings and mobile homes. You will probably find the closing costs lower on this type of loan. Usually, it is $50 or 1%, whichever is more. This covers the credit report, appraisal fee and closing agent's fee. Of course, your buyer will still have his first year's insurance, tax escrow, etc., to pay. The interest rate will be the same as a regular VA loan. The buyer or his agent will be required to see that VA gets the credit report, employment verifications, cover letters, deposit verifications and ordering of the appraisal. VA will be happy to send you the necessary forms and instructions. If anything is not clear to you, don't hesitate to call your local VA office. They will be very helpful. To save time, you should always have a set of these forms available to you in your office. VA will usually issue new forms each time you submit an application. If your buyer is required to go to the VA office to complete any forms, make sure he knows what to do and what not to do.

VA-ACQUIRED HOMES

VA-acquired homes are homes that VA has repossessed and retaken title on. They can be easy sales for any real estate agent. We have always found these homes to be a good market and beneficial to the sales people for several reasons.

First, they are available to anyone to sell. VA does not want to deal directly with the buyer, because of the paperwork and communication necessary. They will advertise for an interested party to contact the broker of his choice.

Office policy usually allows for the salesman and the broker to split the commission 50%-50%, which, by eliminating the listing agent, pays each party a good commission, even though VA only pays a 5% commission on the sale. Very few offices concentrate on these homes because they are too busy worrying about the listings they already have. This means less competition.

Second, VA will usually sell these homes on land contract. If the home has been on the market for a long period of time, they will even offer the home with no down payment, even to nonveterans. They are not terribly strict about qualifying the purchaser, since they are anxious to move the property. The closing costs generally run about 2% of the price of the home. This includes the first year's insurance, prorated taxes, credit report and $25 closing fee. The transaction is handled by mail and closed in the selling broker's office. This type of closing will take 3 to 5 weeks and your commission check is issued after VA receives the signed closing package.

VA will not negotiate on the price or terms. It must be sold as advertised. They may reduce the price if the property does not sell, but it will do you no good to submit a lower offer than the advertised selling price. Call VA and ask them to mail you the necessary forms to submit an offer, so you will have them available to you when you need them. Your broker must have on file with VA a nondiscrimination form before they will deal with you. VA will send you mailings on homes in your area that are for sale. We have even advertised these homes in our office's line ads. It is perfectly legal and will generate numerous floor duty calls, if handled properly. Put the homes that you receive information on in your schedule for inspection during your tour of homes. See what they consist of, so you can talk intelligently about these homes when discussing them with prospects. These homes almost always have keylocks on them or the local property manager (usually another broker) will have the key. If you do not have a VA keylock key, request one from VA or the local property manager.

ATTRACTING A PLENTIFUL SUPPLY OF VA BUYERS

There is a way to develop a VA clientele, not different in many respects from developing buyers in general. The most important thing to remember is to ask each and every prospect, friend, business acquaintance, seller or anyone else you meet, if he or she is a veteran. Many times they will answer "yes," or "no, but my brother is." If the answer is "yes," start talking real estate. Many veterans have no desire to buy a house until they discover what you can do for them on VA.

A man may have $15,000 equity in his home. Why would he want to use VA? Because he can get 100% financing and use his equity to purchase a business, send his kids to college, buy an investment property or put his equity in the bank. Once he discovers the lower interest rate on VA, he may even want to buy a new home.

Another time VA would be handy is when your seller wants to buy another home, but has not sold his present home. By financing with VA, he doesn't need the equity from his present home to complete the purchase.

HOW ONE MAN USED VA TO FINANCE HIS DAUGHTER'S EDUCATION

I once had a client who was looking for a way to use his equity in an apartment building to finance his daughter's last year of college. He had not owned the building very long but had gotten an excellent buy on it. Similar buildings in the neighborhood were selling VA and FHA for $19,000 to $21,000. He had paid only $13,500 for it a few months back and financed the property on a blanket mortgage. We discussed the possibility of selling the property and felt it would be best to sell FHA or VA since they were appraising the properties at much higher than the local lending institutions. The

problem was that it would take time to market an investment property at top dollar.

I studied the problem and the possibilities and decided it would
be best for my client to refinance his own property on VA. He needed
$6,000 within five weeks. The bank would settle for an $11,000
payment to release the apartment building from the blanket mortgage. VA or FHA were the most likely prospects for financing the
building, since it had been appraised conventionally for $6,000 less
than we needed. FHA would require 100-amp wiring, which the
building did not have, and the owner was a veteran and had been
thinking about using his VA anyway.

We took the amount required by the bank to release the mortgage, the closing costs on the new loan, and the amount he needed
for his daughter to make the requested loan amount total. Some minor alterations were necessary to make it qualify for VA. It was set up
as three apartments with two sleeping rooms. This presented two
problems—one: that totalled five units, and VA would only guarantee
four units; two: each apartment was required to have plumbing in
the kitchen and bathroom. The sleeping rooms didn't have a kitchen
or bathroom, let alone plumbing. For appraisal purposes, we made
each of the sleeping rooms part of another apartment. The borrower
had to show intent to live in the property, so we got a letter from
someone stating that he was to rent the owner's former residence.
This gave us more income and explained what he was going to do
with his present home. VA approved the loan without any difficulty.
My client was extremely happy as he got the funds he needed and he
didn't have to pay a capital gains tax that he would have had to pay
if he had sold the property.

BEING CREATIVE WITH VA

This method of using VA can be helpful in selling real estate as
well as releasing equity. Let's assume you have a property that is in
need of repair. No lender will loan any kind of good percentage on
the property. Your seller is unwilling to sell the property on a long-
term contract. If you can locate a VA buyer, you can sell him the
property on a short-term contract. He can fix the property up and
borrow enough money on VA to pay off the contract, get reimbursed
for the expense of remodeling, and pay his closing costs. You can
even secure an appraisal in advance to insure the seller against the
buyer's not being able to get a loan when he is ready. All you have
to do is give the appraiser a copy of the plans so he can put a value

on the property now, that would reflect the value of the property after the remodeling is done. VA will not loan the money until the work is done and a reinspection has been made. There are other times when refinancing a property already owned by your client can help you earn a commission—to release funds to purchase a business or investment property perhaps. The point is, anything can be done with VA, if you know how to use it.

I have had clients who bought a home, got in trouble and were forced to sell it. VA helped these people two ways. First, since they could get 100% financing, they were able to price the home at a good figure to move quickly. Second, VA was less strict on their credit so they were able to purchase another home. It was probably the only method they had available to them to buy another property.

ADVERTISING FOR VA BUYERS

I have found the best way to recruit VA buyers is to advertise for them. An ad something like this will bring a good response from VA buyers:

VETERANS — No money down, not even closing costs on this charming southside ranch with partial basement. Two bedrooms, bath, living room, new kitchen and good schools. If you have been told you cannot buy a home because of credit, lack of down payment, or income, you probably haven't talked to ABC Realty. Call today to see what we can do for you.

You might want to advertise the lower interest rate, 30 years to repay or the benefit they are entitled to, since many veterans have no idea what is available to them. It is a good idea to advertise the fact that veterans can now use their VA more than once. Few veterans know this. Most think a $25,000 eligibility allows them to buy a $25,000 house. Don't educate them too well, though. Just tell them enough to show how little they know and how much you know.

The local American Legion Post or VFW can supply you with a list of veterans in your area. A letter sent to these people explaining a little about what they can buy will produce results. If you are a veteran, frequent these places. Get to know these veterans so they might call you when they think about buying a home. The veteran is instructed to record his DD 214 when he is discharged from service. This is to protect him against loss of his discharge papers. Go to the

county courthouse and spend a few hours reviewing the records.
Compile a list of veterans and match it against your cross-reference
or directory. Once you have the names, addresses and phone num-
bers of the veterans, you can start making contacts. VA and FHA do
not keep records on rejected buyers, just houses. If you know someone who has been rejected or you have a source at a mortgage company you can depend on for leads, contact these people, correct the
problem, find them a new home, and file a new application. Sometimes it is best not to use the same mortgage company, but that
depends on the attitude of the mortgage company itself.

One of your best sources for VA buyers will be the veterans you
have worked with in the past. They will be happy to refer business to
you and quite often know several veterans interested in buying a
home. Remember, most veterans do not know what they have available to them, so don't expect them to come running to you to buy a
home. You have to make them aware of what you can do.

Putting "G.I.'s, No money down" inserts in your signs will produce several leads, since most sales come from your signs. The space
is there, so use it to your advantage.

On top of everything else, your best source for VA buyers is your
competition who has rejected the buyers. Some people just never
learn.

FINANCING MOBILE HOMES WITH VA

VA does guarantee loans on mobile homes that meet the minimum requirements of VA. In order to qualify, the mobile home must
be at least one year old prior to application. The appraisal will include ascertaining each used mobile home unit's compliance with
the VA minimum property requirements for used mobile homes as set
forth in the list following. Each unit appraised will be carefully
viewed inside and outside, including the undercarriage. The remaining physical life, rather than the economic life, will be estimated—the
condition of the mobile home and the value of the appliances. VA
will be very strict about the value placed on furniture.

VA will issue a Certificate of Reasonable Value for units determined to be acceptable under the criteria shown below. CRV's will
be issued on an "as is" basis if at all possible, but in case of extensive
repairs, they will reject the home rather than order these repairs. No
substitutions of furnishings or appliances will be permitted by VA
after the appraisal has been made. The validity period of any CRV for
used mobile homes will not exceed three months, because of the

quick depreciation of mobile homes. The maximum loan term cannot exceed the loan allowed for new mobile homes; single wide, 12 years; double wide, 20 years. All inspections must be done by licensed mobile home repairmen. The mobile home must have the following items:

1. Each room designed for sleeping purposes must have at least one window that can be operated from inside without the use of tools, unless it has an outside door.
2. Must have minimum of two outside doors located at some distance from each other.
3. Must have acceptable automatic smoke detectors installed outside each sleeping room.
4. Single wide units must be a minimum of 10 feet wide and have a minimum floor area of 400 square feet. Double wide units must be at least 20 feet wide when combined. Tip-outs don't qualify single wides as doubles.
5. Must be so constructed as to be towed on its own chassis and/or undercarriage.
6. The unit must contain living facilities for year-round occupancy of a single family, including permanent provisions for heat, sleeping, cooking and sanitation.
7. The unit must be weathertight and habitable from the standpoint of safety, sanitation and structural soundness.
8. VA will require dealers/sellers to warrant used mobile homes.
9. Site location must meet VA standards.
10. If double wide unit is involved and the lot is now or is to be leased, a copy of the lease must be sent to VA with the application. The lease must be for no less than three years and have a provision that allows for the lease to be assumed if the mobile home is sold. The lease may not provide for cancellation without cause.
11. No manufacturer's invoice is required.
12. When the seller of a used mobile home unit is an individual or party other than a dealer/seller, the loan must be submitted on a prior approval basis. Only dealers can get automatic loans.

VA will allow the following charges to be included in the loan: the actual charges for recording, any documentary stamp tax, local and state tax, insurance premium up to five years, and will allow the buyer to pay more than the appraisal, if paid in cash. Setup and transportation charges, and any other closing costs or prepaids incident to real estate involved, cannot be included in the loan.

You should check with your mortgage company for the maximum loan amount in effect at the time for different types of mobile homes. Single wides, double wides and mobile homes with land all have different maximum lending amounts. The interest rate will usually run 5 to 6% higher than the rate for normal VA loans. Your biggest difficulty will be finding a lender willing to make a loan on a mobile home, because of its mobility. Your best bet will be to check with a mobile home dealer as to where he gets his financing. Your local VA could also tell you who has been processing loans through them on mobile homes. Financing a mobile home is one of the most difficult VA loans to work out. Check out what can be done before writing an offer.

DOCUMENTATION NEEDED TO SUPPLEMENT A CREDIT REPORT

I-0- It will be necessary for the buyer to contact the credit grantor and obtain a letter stating date of sale, when first payment is due, current balance, and whether or not payment was received on time. Any past credit history could also be given.

I-2- It will be necessary for the buyer to obtain a letter from the credit grantor stating that the account is now current. It might be well to send along a receipt showing the delinquent payment remitted, and also a letter from the buyer explaining why he was behind on payment.

*I-3- Same as above.

*I-4- Same as above.

*I-5- Same as above.

*I-7- Often this is an unacceptable situation.

*I-8- If a deficiency balance remains, it must be paid. The buyer must write a letter explaining this situation. (If this is a disputed account, it can sometimes be handled differently.)

*I-9- If the collection is still owing, it must be paid. A letter of explanation must be written by the buyer.

*** I-3 thru I-9 — The fewer the better.

*A good reasonable explanation is necessary; documented proof of layoff, illness, etc.

POINTS TO REMEMBER ON VA

1. No down payment needed.
2. VA benefits for real estate loans have *not* expired for anyone originally entitled.
3. All closing costs and prepaids can be paid by the seller.
4. A veteran can use his VA entitlement as many times as he wishes or until his eligibility is used up. If VA loan is repaid, his eligibility is reinstated.
5. VA is more liberal on buyer and house than most other methods.
6. VA will approve buyers with past bankruptcy, collections or credit problems.
7. Certain widows of veterans are entitled to their husband's benefits.
8. Any money that can be verified through letters or employment verifications can be used for income.
9. A veteran can refinance his own property.
10. A veteran receiving a dishonorable discharge can appeal for his benefits.
11. Some lending institutions will approve the loan without submission to VA.
12. VA will permit up to 30 years to repay loan.
13. You can appeal a rejection and your client can personally visit or call VA.
14. You can appeal an appraisal and present evidence of why you feel it should be raised.
15. Apartment buildings, farms, new homes, older homes, mobile homes, as well as normal residences can be financed VA.
16. The veteran can pay more than the appraised amount for a home.
17. You can improve your buyer's credit and income position by writing letters.
18. Two people living together, one veteran and one nonveteran, divorced people, married, can buy VA.

LETTERS TO BE USED IN SUPPORT OF
APPLICATIONS

Mr. John Doe
Indiana Mortgage Company
111 Indiana Avenue
Indianapolis, IN 46200

Dear Mr. Doe:

At your request, I am writing to explain my slow credit rating
and the collection on my credit report. I have always made an
honest effort to keep my payments up-to-date. Until recently, I
was able to do so. My daughter has been ill and required a great
deal of medical attention. My insurance did not cover most of the
expense. Her care was the most important thing and it was, unfortunately, necessary to let my payments slip behind. I have since
been able to bring my payments up-to-date and pay off the medical bills.

The collection that shows on my record was a television set
that we had repaired and that still did not work. I refused to pay
the bill until the set was fixed properly. Instead of fixing it, the
company turned the account over to the credit bureau. As you can
see by this receipt, I gave in and paid the bill.

I apologize for these marks on my record, but hope the circumstances causing this situation and my past good credit record
will make up for it. I hope this will not keep me from getting the
home, as it is closer to work, large enough for my family and will
make my children more secure in having a home of their own.

Thank you for the help you have given me in processing my
application. If you have any further questions, please call me.

Sincerely,

Mike Jones

Using the same format, these letters can be used as a guide
when having someone write a reference or rent letter for your buyer.

Mr. John Doe
Indiana Mortgage Company
111 Indiana Avenue
Indianapolis, IN 46200

Dear Mr. Doe:

I am writing in regard to my bankruptcy in 1971. My wife filed for divorce and ran up bills in our names. I had been giving her the money to pay our debts, but she was spending it instead. With the cost of the divorce, loss of her income, and her spending sprees, I was unable to cope with the debts. I tried to work out an equitable payment schedule with my creditors, but was unable to do so. I was young, upset over the divorce and when my attorney suggested bankruptcy, I thought it was the best thing to do.

I have since remarried and established a good credit record. My wife has helped with the budget and we have worked hard to regain our credit. I hope that our recent record, and the fact that I have a good job, and my honest desire to provide a home for my family, will cause you to rule favorably on my application.

I would like to thank you for the help you have given me and the effort you have made.

Sincerely,

Thomas Smith

Letter from Lender on Slow Credit

Please be advised that Mr. Mike Jones has been a customer of ours for some time and has been a good credit risk. We understood his recent lateness of payment and don't hesitate to recommend him for a loan.

Sincerely,

Jim Wikson, Manager
Acme Finance

Letter from Landlord

Mike Jones has rented a house from us for the past two years. Not only does he keep his rent paid, but he also takes very good care of the property. I would recommend Mr. Jones highly as a creditworthy individual.

Sincerely,

Jim Smith

Letter of Intent to Rent

I now rent an apartment at 206 N. 18th Street. I pay $120.00 per month and plan on staying as long as I am allowed.

Sincerely,

Mary Moore

Letter to Show Credit

Mr. Jones has had an account with my store for the past year and a half. He always pays me on time. I recommend him, without hesitation, as a good credit risk.

Sincerely,

John Jenkins
Jenkins Grocery

Each collection or slowness should be explained. The reason for each might be the same, or there might be a series of extenuating circumstances. Make them logical, and not too terrible, since you don't want them to question whether the problem is cleared up or not. Never type these letters and never use your office's stationery. A letter in a buyer's personal handwriting is more effective.

TAPPING INTO A CONSISTENT FLOW OF SALES

VA is good for your buyers, for your sellers, and it is good for you. If you do your homework correctly, you can cut the processing time down to four weeks, and if your client and property are strong, you can have the loan pre-approved without submission to VA in two weeks. That is not too long to wait for a commission that you probably could not have earned otherwise. VA financing can add ten sales or more each year to your income, if you will learn where to find VA buyers and how to finance them. Once you start to look, you won't believe how many men and women have been in the service. Your attitude towards VA buyers is more important than the knowledge of how to finance them. You have to want to sell VA and look for any opportunity to do so.

CHAPTER FIVE

Financing Business and Commercial Property

Business and commercial property sales can provide you with larger commissions than any other type of sale. Normally, the commission rate is higher on this type of property, a willing buyer is almost always available, and usually you will have an opportunity to earn additional commissions as a result of your commercial sale. Of course, the selling price alone on commercial property makes the extra effort required worthwhile. While commercial sales are not difficult to get into, most agents stumble when they attempt to raise the mortgage funds for their buyer. In this chapter we'll discuss how you can overcome this problem and be as effective in securing commercial capital as the most experienced commercial agent.

COMMERCIAL LOANS AND THE AVERAGE SALESPERSON

Selling commercial property can be very frustrating for the average real estate salesperson. However, it is not difficult to get an interested party, since many people want to own a business of their own. After all, it is the American dream. Owning your own business is a way of getting ahead of the game, and there are always individuals ready to strike out on their own. The commissions are usually large and alluring to an agent. Most commercial property brings a higher commission not only because of the sales price, but also because a higher percentage is charged on commercial transactions. It certainly would seem as if you could afford to put a few extra hours into a sale that might generate more than you would normally earn selling four or five residential properties.

With these two factors combined, one might ask, "What is the problem?" There are two problems, actually—the buyer's lack of money and the seller's opinion of what his property is worth. Most agents spend countless hours spinning their wheels with clients who have a desire to do something without the means to achieve their goal. The average person wanting to buy a business has little experience in the field he chooses and no money to speak of. Those who have money are probably already in some sort of business and the real estate agent on the street seldom gets to deal with them.

The people we deal with are mostly of the first kind, thus it is necessary to know when you have a buyer who can earn you a commission and when you don't. To do this, you must know what can be done and what financing is available on different types of operations. What is required of a borrower to make a lender look favorably on an application? How much does experience count? How important is an accurate operating statement? If you know the answers to these questions, you have a better chance of getting financing on businesses and cutting down on wasted time and effort.

WORKING WITH COMMERCIAL BUYERS AND SELLERS

Before considering the second problem you face when selling commercial property, let's expand on the problem of working with buyers on commercial transactions. Too many salespeople are lured into approaching a commercial client without putting the transaction in its proper perspective. Before they realize it, they have put six months into a commercial sale and let their residential sales slide. At the beginning, it appeared that the transaction would be worth the extra effort because of the bigger reward. Now they have lost $6,000 in sales to make a $3,000 commission. They can't give up now, because they have too much invested in time and lost sales. They're caught in a trap. For the average salesperson, residential sales are the bread and butter of the business. Commercial sales are just a bonus and should be treated as such.

Once you make up your mind to tackle a large transaction, set aside a certain number of hours per day or week to work on it, and stick to your schedule. Arrange your schedule so that you spend the least productive hours of each day putting the package together. Don't depend on the large commission so much that you have to make it work. If you spend the commission before you get it, you will be forced to let your everyday business slide to try to close on the commercial property as quickly as possible. In this case, it's true that "haste makes waste." You must be in a position to use finesse on the lenders, not pressure. A lender once told me that he could give me a quick answer, but if I wanted a "yes," I would have to give him time to evaluate the application. Don't urge the lender to give you an answer quickly; that in itself can cause him to reject the application.

The second problem is even harder to solve. How do you get the seller to ask a reasonable price for his business and give you the necessary figures to prove income? How do you even decide what a reasonable price is? What type of income must a business show to justify the price to the buyer and lender? What do you use as a guideline to determine the value of a business? Most buyers will want to see at least 25% of the purchase price returned annually as a net figure.

Keeping this figure in mind, it should be simple to determine the marketable price for a business. If the seller is unwilling to give accurate, documented figures on the business, or is unwilling to put the business on the market at a figure in line with a return expected by buyers, you are in trouble before you begin.

Now that you are aware of the reasons for not getting involved with commercial property, don't feel that I'm trying to get you to stay out of the commercial market. I am very much in favor of the average salesperson becoming involved, but he must know his limitations going in and be prepared to handle the transaction properly. Commercial sales are exciting, interesting and rewarding; if worked properly, they can be not only an interesting challenge but also a nice addition to your income. I stress the pitfalls of this type of selling because I've seen salespeople walk right into the same trap time after time. They always think this one will be different, but it never is because they never change their approach to the transaction. Sell commercial property, but take it in stride. If this type of selling is not your principal livelihood, don't forget what is and what will continue to be after the closing.

I once had a salesman who spent six months trying to put a farm sale together. He had a buyer, but no seller. He never did find a farm, but he spent six months—unproductive months—talking to farmers, telling himself that when he did find a farm, he would make up for all the lost income over the past six months. Not only did he not sell the farm, but he didn't sell anything else during that six months.

Commercial sales will be rewarding only if you take them in stride, remembering to work with the FHA buyer who has kept you in business in the past. Your check may seem a pittance compared to the commission you are anticipating on the big sale, but it is much more certain of getting into your pocket.

ELEVEN POINTS YOU SHOULD KNOW
ABOUT THE SELLER

Before going into the different aspects of financing businesses, let's take a look at what information you should possess in order to talk honestly and intelligently to a buyer and (we hope), sooner or later, a lender. At the time you list the business, you will not know what method of financing will be required, since you won't know the buyer's circumstances. For this reason, you should have all information available. If you collect all the data you can at the time you secure the listing, you will be prepared for all the buyer's questions, as well as for any type of financing that will later be required.

Following is a discussion of information and an explanation of where to get the information that you should have in marketing and financing a business. It is important that this date be accurate and that you feel certain it is accurate. If a buyer "loses his shirt" because of faulty information or figures, you will be the one he blames for his failure. While some of this information may not seem pertinent to financing, you'll find, when discussing a loan with a lender or when determining the most suitable type of financing, that all of it is vital.

Assets

Obtain a complete list of equipment, fixtures, real estate, inventory and supplies that will be included in the sale. The age, condition and value of each should also be listed. It is best to have these assets appraised by someone in the area who is familiar with the type of equipment involved. This will not only show a buyer what he is getting, but also give credence to the value you place on these items when making a loan application. Most lenders will require a competent appraisal; you can save yourself time by having it in advance.

Profit and Loss Statements

These should be no older than 90 days from the current period. You should also have at least the previous two years' statements to verify the figures given on the current statement. If the business involved has a printout sheet, this will be a very simple matter. If not, the owner's accountant should prepare the statements from the seller's figures and attest to their correctness. An up-to-date audit is always the best method of proving the income figures given by the seller.

Although the seller may not be willing to go to this expense or trouble, the lender is almost sure to ask for this proof; therefore it might as well be done in advance, so the buyer can also have the information. One thing to remember is that a P & L, attested and prepared by an accountant with the notation, "Prepared Without Audit," is not worth the paper it is written on, as far as proof is concerned. The accountant is saying that if the figures given him are true, the P & L is true; it looks impressive, but doesn't help your buyer.

Balance Sheets

A balance sheet is a schedule of the business's assets and liabilities. To the average buyer, they don't mean much. He looks at the bottom line and says, "Sure enough, the assets match the liabilities." What it should reflect, and what the lender will be looking for, is how the seller is making and spending his money. The profit and loss will not show any hidden debts. If there are debts that have not been paid and will be coming due, the income from the P & L may not be as good as it looks. You should have at least the previous two years' balance sheets available.

Federal Income Tax Statements

At least the past two years' income tax filings should be at your disposal. A seller who was really sharp and a little dishonest could file taxes on more money than he actually made in order to use the filings as proof of income. It would cost him some money for a couple of years, but his business would be worth thousands of dollars more when he sold it. I point this out to make you aware that no data is guaranteed to be accurate. Fortunately, most businessmen are honest, and few anticipate selling their business two years in advance. Most lenders will request the tax statements, since they are more likely to be accurate than a profit and loss statement.

Accounts Receivable

A verified list of all accounts receivable and the timeliness of payment on these accounts is important. The buyer and lender will want to know how much money is lost each year on uncollectable accounts, how much of the income is carried on the books, and what type of cash flow the business has. If it is important for a new buyer to have a good cash flow, he must know how much of the income he can expect to carry on paper, even for a short time.

History of Business

You should obtain a brief history of the length of time the business has been in operation, its past successes and failures, the type of clientele, the reason for its success or failure, and an idea of the potential offered a new owner.

Traffic Count

If drive-in traffic or location is important to the operation, a traffic count should be obtained. The city, county, or state should have this information available. If not, you can spend a few hours counting cars; I have.

Zoning

The zoning is of utmost importance. If the property is in a greenbelt area or under a special use permit, you must make sure your buyer is aware of it. This factor could make a big difference in the future expansion of the business.

Percentage of Profit

Depending on the type of business you are in, it may be necessary to break down the percentage of profit into individual items. In manufacturing, knowing how much of the income is spent in production, how much in shipping, and how much in overhead, can show the buyer ways to improve the profit picture and serve as a guideline to him concerning what the business should be doing. In some operations only the net percentage will be needed. This will immediately indicate whether the return on the purchase price is good or bad.

OSHA

Something that is overlooked by many buyers is whether the company is subject to federal safety regulations, and if it is, does the business meet those standards? If a firm does not meet minimum safety requirements, several thousand dollars may have to be paid by the new owner, unexpectedly, to bring the equipment or building up to minimum safety standards.

Reason for Selling

The first question I am always asked is "why is the seller selling, if it such a good business?" Not only do the buyers wonder, but the lenders are also concerned about why the business is being sold. If the reason is not health, retirement, another business venture or some other solid reason, you should also wonder. If you can't convince yourself, you'll not convince the buyer or lender.

As with any listing, you should have the lot size, square footage of building, type of construction, pictures, etc. If you get this information in advance, you will save time and embarrassment later. If you have to go back to the seller every time the buyer or lender requests new information, you will eventually upset the seller, make the buyer wonder why you don't know these things, and delay the lender's decision. Do it right the first time and you'll have a better idea of what you're dealing with, what problems you must overcome and in the long run, save a lot of shoe leather.

Financing the Buyer

I can't tell you that a certain method of financing will work for a particular type of buyer. Selecting financing is not that easy and you must learn to be flexible with commercial financing. In this section you will learn what is available with this kind of financing and how to obtain it, but you will have to decide which method will work for each transaction after studying your buyer's circumstances. Making this decision won't be as difficult as it might sound because your buyer's situation will eliminate most choices. Your most important step is to choose the best avenue as soon as possible, so that you don't get your client out of the mood of buying and tie up too much of your time with one closing.

UTILIZING THE SMALL BUSINESS ADMINISTRATION AS A VITAL COMMERCIAL MONEY OUTLET

SBA is a governmental agency designed to help small businesses secure financing for expansion, purchase, construction, or refinancing. They will also offer consultation in any area in which the businessman feels a need for assistance. Those qualifying for SBA assistance must fall into certain categories. They are as follows:

1. Businesses independently owned and operated and not dominant in their field.
2. Those unable to obtain private financing under reasonable terms.
3. Those not eligible for financing from other governmental agencies.
4. Those qualified as "small" under SBA size standards based on dollar volume or number of employees.

The maximum loan available under this program varies, depending on the percentage of SBA involvement. The maximum amount SBA will participate in, guarantee, or loan directly is $350,000. Thus, if SBA is taking 50% of a participation loan or guarantee, the maximum would be $700,000. The interest rate on these loans will also vary, depending on the current market rate charged by the lender involved. SBA will allow legal and reasonable interest to be charged by the lender, but may place a ceiling on the rate from time to time.

If the loan is a direct loan from SBA, the interest rate will normally be less than that charged by local lenders. As a rule, SBA allows a 10-year maximum maturity. A working capital loan, however, is usually limited to 6 years, while a construction loan may have a maximum of 15 years. It is possible to negotiate with SBA on the maturity of the loan involved.

SBA will accept real estate or chattel mortgages, as well as assignment of warehouse receipts, certain kinds of contracts, guarantees, or personal endorsements as collateral for these loans. In some cases, assignment of current accounts receivable can be used.

It is important to understand the basic idea behind the Small Business Administration in order to secure financing assistance from them. SBA was set up to help small businessmen establish and maintain a business, in the belief that small businesses are important to our economy and that they can easily be overrun by larger companies if not given assistance from time to time. SBA is concerned with making small businesses successful so that they can compete with the larger companies. This is good for everyone, whether involved with small businesses or not. As long as a man or woman has an opportunity in this country to establish and maintain a business of his or her own and provide a product or service that is worthwhile, we as consumers, as well as business people, will benefit.

This competition keeps the quality high and the prices competitive, and allows us to keep the belief that this is still a country of opportunity which allows an individual to attain whatever heights his or her ability will permit. Knowing this and understanding why SBA is available will help you present your application in the best light.

The first requirement for obtaining SBA's assistance in either a participation loan, guarantee program, or direct loan is that the borrower has been turned down by a local lender. If the community has a population of over 200,000, two lenders must provide a letter stating that they will not loan your client the necessary funds. The idea behind this, of course, is that SBA wants to help only those businesses that have no other means of securing financing. You will soon discover that getting a loan turned down is the easiest part of the transaction; we all have a knack for that.

Second, an SBA application and accompanying forms must be completed by the applicant. Many banks will have these forms available, or you can write or call SBA and they will send you the necessary forms and instructions for completion. SBA does not allow for paying an unreasonable fee in connection with the preparation of the application and closing. They will, of course, permit the collection of your commission on the sale of the business and reasonable attorney fees.

When you begin your application, you may not know what kind of assistance you want or can get from SBA. As mentioned earlier, you must be turned down by a local lender to get SBA help. At that point, you have the participation loan, direct loan or guarantee loan to use. The one you choose will probably be the one SBA or the lender tells you is available. If it is a participation loan, SBA will issue their part of the funds and the lender will issue his part. If it is a loan guarantee, the lender and SBA will agree on the amount of the loan to be guaranteed by SBA. If it is a direct loan, SBA will loan the entire amount to the borrower without the involvement of a lender.

The difficulty with the participation loan and direct loan programs is that SBA usually runs out of money long before their fiscal year is up. This means the majority of loans you will work on with SBA will be on the loan guarantee program.

You may find that some banks are not very willing to become involved with SBA on business loans. The reason this attitude exists among some lenders is that SBA does not guarantee loans as we are used to with FHA or MGIC. They guarantee a percentage of the loan, but not the top percent. In other words, if their guarantee is 15% of the loan and there is a $5,000 loss to be taken, SBA takes only 15% of the loss, rather than the top 15% of the loan. Losing only 85% of their money does not appeal to many lenders. The lender is required to review the application, run the credit check and appraise the collateral. SBA is almost totally dependent on the lender for the screening of the application—if the lender approves the loan, SBA usually will. Depending upon the area in which you are working, SBA is usually very good about moving on the applications quickly. You can plan on two weeks for approval or rejection from the time SBA receives the application.

SBA usually wants something from the borrower involved in the loan. They will normally ask to see 20% of the purchase price down, or that much equity in a business presently owned by the borrower. When looking at a borrower, they are looking for credit worthiness, ability, business experience in the field they are financing, a good business record, and honesty. I have found the most successful kind of client to have when dealing with SBA is one with experience in the field he is going into, preferably in the actual business being purchased, and one who has good credit.

When filling out the application and documents for SBA, make them as complete and sensible as possible. The first form required is a request for SBA consultation; they want to know in what area the individual needs the most help. When filling this form out, choose an area that is sincere, yet does not show poor ability to operate a business. Ask for help in using effective advertising and spending advertising dollars. It is an area in which most people could use help, yet it does not indicate any lack of good business sense.

Tell them what they want to hear. The way to do this is to imagine yourself on the other side of the fence. What would you want to see in a borrower if you were an officer of SBA? Probably knowledge, credit, sincerity, experience, capital, conservatism, and confidence are among your wants. Show these things when you are compiling the information for SBA. Before completing the forms or producing income figures, always ask yourself, "What would make sense to me and make me like this person as a borrower?" Answer all questions honestly and completely.

You will be required to fill out an estimated projection of income for the next two years. This form should show a well-thought-out plan for increasing the profit picture, and it should be a realistic plan. Many times the payment on an SBA loan and the maturity will be based on the amount of money left as the net figure on the projection sheet. Make sure the figure you arrive at as a projected net is large enough to show SBA a means of repayment. All of the forms that must be filled out for SBA will seem long and complicated, but they really are not. If you follow the instructions, the application will be fairly simple to complete.

There are other kinds of SBA loans available besides small business loans. There are economic opportunity loans, which are basically the same as business loans except that they are aimed at individuals who have low incomes or are disadvantaged, who have lacked the opportunity to start and maintain a small business, and who cannot secure the funds from other sources on reasonable terms. The maximum amount available is $50,000 for SBA's share of the loan. There are loans for state and local development companies, loans to small business investment companies and to licensees organized solely to assist disadvantaged entrepreneurs, as well as disaster loans. SBA will maintain communication with the businessman throughout the duration of the loan. They will always be ready to assist the borrower in any area where he feels a need for improvement. I have found the individuals at SBA to be cordial, willing to help, and wanting to make a loan to a deserving businessman.

USING CONTRACTS FOR EVERYONE'S PROFIT

Chapter Nine discusses contracts and assumptions at length; however, the following section is included here specifically for businesses and commercial property. If a seller is in a position to sell on contract and use the monthly payments as income, there will be no problem. Contracts, however, can be used for short-term financing while arranging financing with a commercial lender. The contract would call for a payoff in six or twelve months with extensions if suitable financing could not be arranged.

Another method of using contract financing is to provide for the purchase of certain parts of a business under contract and allowing the down payment to cover the remainder. This will leave you an asset for the buyer to use as collateral, so that he might raise his down payment money. Since it is impossible, without knowing the particulars of a purchase, to foresee every circumstance that will arise, I cannot list specific instructions on what should be contained in the contract. It must suffice to say that you, as an agent for a buyer or seller, must foresee all difficulties that might arise and spell these items out in the contract.

There are such things as good will, franchise rights, leases, quality of product and public relations that must be considered. If a house is repossessed, it does not hurt the character or salability of the property. If a business is shut down for a month while a default is being made, the business can be ruined. No matter how good the business is, the stigma of closing down and the loss of customers will hurt it to such a degree that the original owner might not recover his former following. Prepare in advance for a smooth transfer if a default should occur. Leave no doubt about whether you have protected the buyer and seller in all areas.

PACKAGE MORTGAGES

When equipment and real estate are involved in the sale of a business, a package mortgage can be obtained, using the equipment and real estate as collateral. Savings and loans are unable to make this kind of loan, since they can loan only on real estate. This makes banks and commercial lenders your best prospect for borrowing package money. The maturity and interest rate on the loan will be adjusted to combine the rate for equipment loans and real estate loans. If the equipment involved is fairly new and in good condition, your chances of getting a loan with good terms will be greatly enhanced. If your buyer has good credentials and a healthy down payment, a package mortgage will work well. If you need more than 75% or 80% financing, it is best to separate the equipment and real estate, since this allows you more flexibility. For instance, on the sale of a laundromat, you would need to combine a chattel mortgage for the equipment and a real estate loan for the property.

LEASES AND LEASE COMPANIES

Although lease companies will not appear very attractive to a buyer, they can be a very good way to finance a business. If the business involved includes only equipment and good will, using a lease company can get your client 100% financing. The lease company will purchase the equipment from the seller and lease it to the buyer. They require the first three lease payments in advance, but will cover the entire purchase price. Their charge for the money they use to purchase the equipment is high compared to most outlets. If you were to consider it as interest, your buyer might pay as much as 18 to 20%. The maturity will be between five and ten years, depending on the age and condition of the equipment involved. The lessee will be obligated for the maintenance and replacement of the equipment. At the end of the lease period, the lessor will sign it over to the lessee for one dollar. They cannot put this in writing, of course, or they would no longer be considered a lease company.

To qualify for the lease, a lessee must be creditworthy and have a net worth of twice the total of the lease. It will be necessary for you to supply the lease company with an appraisal of the equipment, a credit report on the buyer, and the buyer's financial statement. An appraisal can be obtained from anyone who is qualified, such as a wholesaler, distributor, or manufacturer. If you were dealing with a restaurant, you could get a restaurant equipment supplier to give you his opinion of value. If it is an automotive or parts store, a local parts distributor could be used. It will also be necessary for you to supply the P & L statement to the lease company for the business involved. It should, of course, show that the income is there to make the lease payments.

In most situations, the lease company will not personally see the equipment or meet with the lessee at any point in the transaction, unless the lessor is local. The nice thing about a lease company is that they will come into any area, even one thousands of miles from their office, and if your buyer cannot show a net worth equal to that required, you can use a cosigner.

For example, I listed an automotive store for $15,500. The building was leased, so the purchase price included the equipment and good will only. The inventory was to be sold separately, and the P & L statement showed a good cash flow and a good profit. I had a client who was interested in purchasing a business such as this, but he was relatively young and did not have any money to use as a down payment. We went to a lease company with an itemized list of the equipment involved, its value (which was certified by a local parts distributor) and the necessary information on the business and buyer as well. We asked them to purchase the equipment at the listed price and lease it back to my client over a five-year period. They looked at the P & L to see what type of income could be anticipated and the value of the equipment. Both were satisfactory, but my client's financial statement did not show enough net worth. I arranged for a cosigner on the lease who did have the necessary net worth and they agreed to complete the transaction. By using a lease company I had gotten 100% financing on a business I could not even get the local banks to look at.

If you happen to be selling a building that is leased by a AAA company or a firm that has a good reputation in the community, you can use the lease to secure 100% financing. If you have a building for sale that is leased by an insurance company, for instance, you can take the lease to the bank and get all the money you need as long as the buyer is willing to assign the income to the bank as security.

You can also use a purchase-leaseback as a means of selling and financing property. You have a buyer interested in purchasing an investment property that won't require a lot of attention. You know a businessman in need of some cash. The owner can sell the building to your buyer and lease it back. Because of the lease, you can get excellent financing terms for your buyer.

Purchases and leases can also be used in other instances. I once had a buyer interested in purchasing a lot, constructing a building on it, and operating a business. The buyer was not in a position to handle a transaction of this size, so I had an investment client whom I approached about buying the lot, putting up the building and leasing it back to my buyer. The investor was able to get good terms on the financing because of the lease and the lessee was able to get the property he wanted, when he wanted it. I not only made a commission on the sale of the lot, but also earned a fee for bringing the lessee and lessor together.

I have been involved in transactions that called for the lessor to lease the ground to the lessee, with the lessee erecting the building. The lessee was given credit for lease payments in an amount equal to the cost of the building and interest. The lessee had the style of building he wanted, and the lessor had allowed the lessee to build and pay off a nice commercial building for him.

Many things can be done with leases by tying them with contracts. I once sold a business with the equipment, good will, and inventory being sold on contract and the real estate being leased. The buyer was able to get in with less money down, since he didn't have to purchase the building, and the seller was able to have a reliable source of income for life. It also gave the seller more control over the business, since the contract and lease were tied together in case of default.

Another attractive way to use a lease is to write it for a number of years, allowing the lessee to purchase the real estate at the end of

the lease for a predetermined amount. This allows the buyer to put
equity into a property monthly, rather than having to come up with
a large sum for a down payment. If you keep them in mind, leases
can be very important in selling commercial property. You may have
someone who wants to own a business, but is without the needed
capital. At the same time, you may have someone who has no interest
at all in owning a business, but is interested in making investments.
By combining the two, you earn a commission, and they each have
what they want.

You must not think of leases as the renting of property, but rather as an important financing tool. Leases, like contracts, can be anything you want them to be. They can be long- or short-term and they
can be used to improve the financing terms or to reduce the down
payment. If you have an idea, you can put it in a lease.

CHATTELS

A chattel mortgage is a loan on equipment, and is usually made
by a bank through its commercial loan department. The loan is made
to an owner of equipment, using the equipment for collateral. The
funds derived from this type of financing can be used for the purchase of equipment, or for working capital, or for any other use the
buyer might have for it. If the equipment is in good condition and
you have a decent borrower, a high percentage of the value of the
equipment can be borrowed. The maturity on the loan will depend
on the equipment involved, but will usually not run for more than
ten years.

COMMERCIAL REAL ESTATE LOANS

Depending upon your area and the condition and location of the
property involved, you can anticipate being able to borrow anywhere
from 50% to 80% of the purchase price on a commercial real estate
loan. It is generally difficult to borrow over 75% of the purchase
price. You can expect to pay 1 or 2% more interest than on residential
property and expect a more conservative appraisal. The maturity will
be less than a residential loan also, normally not running more than
15 years.

Since only real estate is involved, you can use savings and loans,
banks, insurance companies, investors, private individuals or finance
companies. The size of the loan will dictate where you take the loan,
at least to a certain point. An insurance company is not likely to loan

on a $50,000 transaction. Some small banks will have a lower ceiling than the amount needed. You must, on each transaction, judge which outlet is the best for the situation you are dealing with.

PUTTING ALL OF THE PIECES TOGETHER TO ENSURE SUCCESSFUL COMMERCIAL FINANCING

You now are aware of the basic outlets for commercial properties: SBA, contracts, leases, package mortgages, chattels, commercial notes and commercial real estate loans. The success or failure of your commercial transactions will depend on your ability to put these different methods together to arrange suitable financing for your buyer. Each method, except leases, requires a good-sized down payment. Since a buyer rarely has this kind of money to put down, you must find some way to raise the percentage of financing that can be obtained. This can be done in many ways, depending upon the circumstances you are involved with.

I once arranged a SBA loan for 80% of the purchase price of a restaurant. The buyer was the manager of the establishment. He had a good credit rating and a solid working knowledge of the restaurant business. We had no difficulty with the loan, but he did not have the required 20% down. We arranged for his father to give him this money, which was fine with the lender involved. The father was, in reality, willing to use his assets to help his son borrow the down payment. We used some stock he owned to borrow the down payment at a very low rate of interest. The son repaid the loan from the proceeds of the business. The father had not cashed in his stock, could still collect his dividends, and had enabled his son to purchase a business.

Another time I sold a commercial building on contract and the equipment for cash. The buyers used the equipment as collateral to borrow the down payment. I have sold commercial property (corporations) on contract with the stock being transferred free and clear. By allowing the down payment to go towards the total cost of the stock, the buyer had an asset to borrow on in order to raise his down payment. He could sell the stock to raise the necessary funds also.

Combining a commercial real estate loan to finance the real estate with the use of a lease company to purchase the equipment is also a means of implementing two methods to finance all or most of the purchase price. By rearranging the selling price in comparison with the value of each, you can raise the amount of money that you would normally be able to borrow. If you use the equity in a buyer's home, you can arrange 100% financing, either through a trade at an inflated price or a new mortgage.

Don't forget trades as a means of financing businesses, by trading either commercial property for commercial property or commercial property for residential property. Trades can do more than reduce capital gains taxes. They can be used to make up the down payment required by trading equity. Equity can be raised or lowered as needed to make the figures come together, by raising or lowering the price of either property.

Financing commercial property requires knowledge of the types of loans available and the outlets for each. More important, it takes an agent who can be original. He or she must be able to bridge the gap between what the buyer has and what he needs. Hopefully, once you know what is available, you will come up with some ideas on how to combine the methods at your disposal to make a transaction work.

PREPARING AND PRESENTING THE APPLICATION

It is important to know the attitude of the institutions you are dealing with. How do they feel about certain types of properties? What do they like to see in a borrower? How flexible are they on their down payment requirements? What type of rapport do you have with them? To be successful at financing commercial properties, you have to know how the lender thinks so that you can present the application in its best light and can choose the right lender for the type of sale you are trying to finance. There is only one way to find the answers to these questions: ask the lenders. Don't find out the hard way, by getting a loan rejected.

As I stated before, it is important, when completing an application, that the information be correct, complete and conservative. A lender will want to know what kind of a profit or loss the business has been showing, what assets are being transferred and the condition of those assets, what type of cash flow is present, how much experience the buyer has, and what his plans are for the future to maintain or increase the profit picture. The way to show the lender the answers to these questions is to have available the information that is listed in the front of this chapter. I have found it wise to have this data, but not to take it to the lender until he requests it. Instead of taking all the material with me on the first visit, I ask the lender what data he will need to reach a decision. No matter how much I make available to lenders at the first meeting, they ask for something else. Lenders have a need to control the situation, and to keep people so busy meeting their demands that they don't have time to question what the lenders are doing. Now they have to tell me what they need at one time. The next day I have it for them and they have no excuse for not acting on the application. There is also a safety feature in operating this way. If you don't give them information they don't need, they won't find something in it that they don't like. Never tell them too much.

The reason the seller is selling is important, but the reason your buyer is buying is also important. How will this purchase improve his situation and is he sure he's making a move for the better? When the buyer talks to the lender, he must be confident he is making the right choice.

It is usually best to arrange for any secondary financing that will be needed in advance, so that you can show the lender where the down payment money is coming from. If your buyer is purchasing a $100,000 business and the requested loan amount is $75,000, the lender will probably be concerned about where the remaining $25,000 is coming from. If you tell him you are hopeful of borrowing it from his competitor across the street, he will probably give you back your application. If you can tell him the down payment is coming from a relative or the money is in the bank or that your client is going to sell an asset, your chances of getting the loan will be much better. There is nothing that scares a lender more than the buyer's not having anything invested in his purchase. The only way I have found to get around this after the lender finds out is to ask for such a low percentage of the purchase price that the lender feels he cannot get hurt.

JUSTIFYING THE AMOUNT OF YOUR LOAN REQUEST

An area that many real estate agents don't put enough effort into is giving credence to the information given a lender. An MAI appraisal cannot be argued with by any lender. If you have equipment involved, get a competent appraisal on it for the use of the lender. Any type of business or equipment can be appraised by the wholesaler for the respective line of merchandise. If you are presenting a P & L, get it certified by an accountant. You may even have to have the business audited. If it is your projection of future income that you're trying to sell them, provide reasonable evidence that supports your figures. Comparisons with other businesses in the same category, projections issued by wholesalers or franchisers, or past increases can all add validity to your figures.

PERSISTENCE AND PATIENCE — THE MAIN INGREDIENTS

Even on solid transactions you will run into problems and time delays. The key to being a success with business and commercial property sales is to be persistent and have patience. Don't give up. If you have thought out the transaction and made the effort to prepare each step wisely, you'll earn that large commission, and you'll be ready to tackle another highly rewarding project.

CHAPTER SIX

Financing Investment Property

Much is written about using leverage when financing commercial and investment property. You can find books that discuss how to increase a client's return by reducing his down payment and increasing his debit service. (For those new to the real estate industry, leverage is the term for purchasing property with as little down payment as possible by borrowing a high percentage of the purchase price.)

To help you better understand leverage, let's discuss the subject in the scope of reality: Every investment buyer either wants or needs to borrow as much mortgage money as you can get for him. It's that simple. Almost every investment buyer you work with will need to finance 95 – 100% of the purchase price. For the most part, if investment buyers had money, they wouldn't want the problems of owning an apartment building. It's great to discuss buyers who have $50,000 or $100,000 to put down on a half-million dollar property, but you and I won't run into many of them, so let's discuss the buyers we will run into—those with no money and a limited income. They are the clients who will make your car payment.

There is a bright side, however. Once you have the ability to provide buyers with 100% financing on investment property, you will never run out of clients. The number of individuals who want to own investment property, but who have little or no funds, is limitless.

A LIMITLESS MARKET FOR COMMISSIONS

Investment properties could be a very good market for most real estate salespeople, if they knew how to finance them. Investment properties are a different breed of cat altogether. They usually are in an undesirable location, in need of repair, and attract buyers with little money. If you have a client interested in a nice apartment building in a good location, your only problem will be in securing his down payment. Most times, however, you will be involved with a property that does not appraise well and a buyer who has little money in the bank to work with and is interested in increasing his income. In other words, you have to be resourceful and aggressive to be successful at selling investment properties.

Before you can finance an investment property, you have to sell it. I won't take up three pages telling you how to sell investment property; I'll leave that to your sales manager. But, I do want to warn you of a fault that many sales people have. For some reason, they have to like a building before they can sell it. It's an investment, not a home. You probably like a Rolls Royce better than a Volkswagen, but whose stock are you going to buy? You have to look at the property as a return on dollars invested. If the income is good and the record of the building has been good, it does not matter how desirable the location is or what conveniences the property has to offer.

One other problem you will constantly have is the buyer not being familiar with investment properties. Most first-time buyers will look at a property the way they would look at their home. They are shocked by the conditions and location of the apartments. You must make them understand that they are not going to live there; they are just going to stop by once a month and collect the rent. Cushion them for the hard facts of investment property ownership. Most owners don't keep their property in the best condition since they bought the building for income and not to see how nice a building they could own. Educate them on what to look for in an investment property. Learn how to compute a capitalization rate, how to estimate vacancies, repairs and increases in utilities. Don't show them only the rate of return on the purchase price, but also the rate of return on the dollars they invest.

CONTRACT FINANCING THAT MAKES BOTH THE BUYER AND SELLER HAPPY

Contract financing is the most flexible and most widely used method of financing investment property. Its use, however, could be even greater if more agents would be more creative when considering how contracts can help them earn a commission. Chapter Nine deals exclusively with using contract and assumption financing, so we won't go into depth on contracts in this chapter, except to present some ideas particular to investment property.

The biggest obstacle to using contract financing successfully is that it does not release the seller's equity. With some ingenuity on your part, you can overcome this obstacle and make both the buyer and seller happy.

Let's look at some examples of how a few creative salespeople used contracts to get the buyer in with little or no down payment and were still able to release the seller's equity:

1. A Houston, Texas saleslady had listed an investment property for $30,000, which was less than the market value of the property. Her client had good credit, but no funds for a down payment. Realizing that the owner could get better financing with investment property than a new buyer, she sold the property on contract with unique terms.

The contract was for the entire $30,000 purchase price, plus $3,000, but was to be paid off in six months. At the end of the six-month period, and after some repairs had been completed, her buyer went to the bank as the owner and borrowed the entire $30,000 using the reasoning with the bank that he could save money, since the contract holder was willing to discount the contract for an early payoff from $33,000 to $30,000. She then collected her commission and both the seller and buyer had what they wanted.

2. A Des Moines, Iowa salesman sold a four-unit apartment building using a contract to provide unique financing for the buyers and earn himself a $1,300 commission. Faced with a buyer who needed to buy on contract and a seller who was

buying the property on contract, he convinced the contract holder to convert the contract to a first mortgage. This allowed the seller to have title and borrow out his equity using a second mortgage. The buyer then bought the building on contract with payments large enough to cover the first and second mortgages.

3. I once had a client who was a speculator. Using contract financing with a 90-day payoff, he turned the property over, paid off the contract and made a profit, thereby earning me two commissions at the same time. The contract gave him more flexibility than an option would since he did own the property, yet allowed him to make a profit without investing his own money.

CONVENTIONAL FINANCING AVAILABLE TO YOUR INVESTMENT BUYER

The two most likely methods of first mortgage money are conventional loans of 75% or less and blanket mortgages. Blanket mortgages work well, particulary if the equity in the other property being offered as security is unquestionable. We won't discuss blanket mortgages in great detail, since they are covered in the chapter on conventional financing, and if you have a situation that offers blanket financing, it won't be that difficult to work out, anyway. At best, depending on the attitude of the banks and savings and loans in your area, you should be looking at 75% financing. At worst, you should be able to obtain 50% financing. I realize that is quite a spread when you are trying to tell a buyer how much he will need for a down payment. Most of the time it won't be that big a problem since your buyer won't have the 25% down if you get him the best financing available. What do you do then? You use your resources and finance yourself a commission.

USING LEVERAGE TO INCREASE YOUR BUYER'S RETURN

Almost everyone wants to use leverage when looking at investment property. This is fine, except that most banks feel that the days of leverage are over. The problem then is how to get the buyer leverage and keep the banks happy at the same time.

The less money your buyer puts down on property, the more

leverage he has. The reasoning behind it is that equity does not pay a return. The more dollars you have tied up in equity, the less return you will receive on your money. Instead of putting $20,000 down on one investment, you should put $4,000 down on five investments, thus increasing the power of your money five times.

The idea is a good one. The only real way to make money is by using someone else's. The tighter money gets, however, the less the banks like investment property. They are, without a doubt, the highest risk, and usually demand a higher rate of return on interest than a residential property. For this reason, you will have to be prepared when you walk into a bank for a loan on a class B apartment building. (That sounds better than calling it a dog.)

PREPARING AND PRESENTING THE APPLICATION

How you present the application will go a long way towards determining the success or failure of the transaction. The old saying, "Banks will only loan you money when they're sure you don't need it," is not far from being true. Take the attitude that you are shopping around for the best lender. Don't discount the fact that how you talk to the lender when securing first or secondary money is important. If you are a good real estate agent, you know how to anticipate the thoughts of buyers and sellers. Do the same thing with the lenders. Know how they think and you will know how to get what you want. You will know what information to give them and what to keep from them.

How do you get to know the lenders and their attitudes? I always made it a practice to invite a different loan officer each month to a sales meeting. In this informal atmosphere you can question him on his attitude and policies, as well as his employer's, on different types of borrowers, properties, and methods of raising down payments. I also take these lending officers to lunch now and then. You'd be surprised how much you can learn about their policies, by just stopping in to visit and being there when the phone rings. Discussing different transactions with your associates will help you understand what has worked for them.

Never present a loan application to a lender, either primary or secondary, and ask if a buyer is allowed to do this or that. It will be obvious that you are trying to find a way to finance the buyer, and if your questions differ from their policies, you will get a rejection. I ask about their policies on certain types of properties or where the down payment can come from before I ever take them a copy of the proposition. This way I know how much to let them in on. Repeating for emphasis, don't lie to the lender, but don't give away information that you don't have to. As they say in the army, "Don't volunteer for anything."

MAKING YOUR LISTING ACCESSIBLE
TO THE APPRAISER

Many loans have been lost because the appraiser or lending officer could not get in to all of the apartments or was accompanied by a tenant who downgraded the property during the entire inspection. In order to prevent these problems from occurring, and to ensure a favorable inspection, have the owner accompany the appraiser. Advise your client to say nothing unless asked a question and to answer each question cautiously.

DON'T GIVE UP!

If the mortgage amount you request is cut, don't burn the bridge behind you. Many times the lender will give a lower than requested commitment just to find an easy way out of the loan. Sometimes the lender doesn't have as much money in his accounts as he would have you think, and, of course, once in a while the property isn't worth more than it is appraised for. I don't let the lender off that easy, however; I tell them I am disappointed, but will see what I can work out. I have closed many transactions where I am sure the lender never thought he would be involved in the loan. I just dig a little more deeply for secondary financing. If the lender turns down the loan altogether, I find out why. If you know why one lender turned down the loan, maybe you can correct the problem before going to the next one.

SEEKING OUT THE RIGHT LENDER

The better your buyer and property are, the less you will have to worry about financing, so let's assume we are dealing with a buyer with average income and credit and a property of class B or less. Knowing where to take the mortgage application is the first obstacle to overcome. You will not get the mortgage the first time on every try, but you should be able to raise your average by selecting a financial institution that has a history of making loans on the type of property that you are selling. I knew of a savings and loan institution that turned down 34 loan applications in less than a year in one particular area. It was obvious they were redlining and it made no sense to bring them a loan application for property in that area. Others will have a minimum price property they will loan on; therefore, where you take the loan application should depend upon where your buyer has a good record and which one loans on the type of property involved.

GIVING THE LENDER A REASON TO MAKE THE LOAN

Give the lender a reason to make the loan. If the income is good, ask the buyer to go along with a higher rate of interest. Present the application, requesting a higher rate of interest than you might normally ask for. Now, at this point, you might say, "Why ask for a higher rate going in? Why not wait for the lender to request a higher rate of interest, so I might get my buyer the lowest rate possible?"

First impressions are important. Do you believe that statement? You probably do, and that's why you make sure your car is clean, your shoes are shined, your hair combed, clothes pressed, and tie straight, or skirt neatly hemmed. Why are first impressions important? People are quick to decide whether they like something or not. No matter what the real circumstances are, if someone gets a bad first impression of you, you are sunk. An opinion has been formed; an attitude has been assumed; it may be impossible to change it.

What does this have to do with financing? Well, imagine you are a lender. A real estate agent brings you an application on a run-down apartment building and asks for the normal 12% interest rate and an 80% loan. Your first impression is, "Boy, this had better be good to get these terms." With that one thought in mind, you subconsciously find every fault you can with the property, because you decided when you took the application that it was going to be tough. You look at the whole picture with that attitude. You scrutinize the buyer and the property. Now, even if you were to get a higher rate, you've found too many faults with the transaction.

Now, let's reverse the circumstances. The going rate for mortgage money is still 12%. A real estate salesperson brings you an application for a 75% loan at 13% interest. Your very first thought is "I'd sure like to make a loan at 13% and show off for the boys upstairs." Being a good employee, you would never loan money that shouldn't be loaned; you would never conceal facts or compromise your position. You would, however, subconsciously, be optimistic about the loan through the processing. You would overlook some minor points, instead of looking for the bad points. The difference, without your even realizing it, (as the officer), is the first impression.

When I call a lender about an offer I am working on, and he tells me he doesn't know whether he can handle it or not, but to bring the buyer in and he'll take a look at it, I know he doesn't want to make the loan before I ever take it to him. He is going to look for ways not to make the loan.

The lender has to remember why he is in the business. If he doesn't loan money, he can't pay interest to his depositors. How many times have you had a transaction foiled because the buyer was not willing to make an offer for a price that you and he both knew it took to buy the property? He wanted to make a low offer and let the seller set the bottom dollar, in hopes of getting the property for just a little bit less. Instead of setting the bottom dollar, the seller took the attitude that the buyer was trying to steal the property and would not negotiate at all. In other words, don't be greedy. Offer the lender a fair rate or a little better than a fair rate, so you might get the buyer the income he desires.

PROVIDING THE LENDER WITH ACCURATE, COMPLETE AND TIMELY INFORMATION

While you will want to wait to present most of the information to the lender until he requests it, you should be prepared to supply the answers when requested. Information you should possess includes:

A. All utility figures for the past 12 months
B. Rental income
C. Cost of repairs in the last 12 months
D. Any recent capital improvements
E. Reason for selling

USING SECONDARY FINANCING TO SELL APARTMENT BUILDINGS AND OTHER INVESTMENT PROPERTIES

How do you use secondary financing to sell apartment buildings and other investment properties? To start, by studying the chapter on secondary financing, you know what can be done with secondary financing to obtain down payment money. Whether you are using a contract or conventional financing, there is a method available to secure the down payment. To know and believe that, in itself, will be a big step in the right direction. When you know there is a way, you will keep looking until you find it. When you are financing investment property and your buyer is going to need more than a 75% loan or secondary financing, you must decide how and where you are going to obtain the money before going into the application.

It is useless to walk into a bank and ask for 90% financing when you know they are only going to give you a 75% loan on any normal investment property. If you arrange for the secondary financing first, you can tell the lender how much your buyer has to work with and how much you need on the first mortgage. The bank is going to question where the down payment is coming from. If the money is in the bank, they won't question how it got there. Also, if you have already lined up the secondary money and the first mortgage comes out for less than anticipated, you can use a different outlet to secure the extra money needed. The buyer and seller are more willing to go along, since you are so close. Let me give you an example.

HOW TO USE A COMBINATION OF FOUR TYPES OF LOANS TO CLOSE A SALE

I had an investment client who was interested in a three-unit apartment building; the selling price was $32,750. We wrote an offer for an 80% loan with 10% down and a 10% pledge from the seller. The seller, who was buying the property on contract, agreed to the terms and accepted the offer. I then set out to secure the 10% down payment for the buyer. On the third try, I succeeded in getting the money on a commercial note. We then made the application for the first mortgage. The lender did not appraise the property high enough for us and I still needed $1,000. The lending officer stated that they would not allow the pledge to be increased and they did not want to see a second mortgage on the property, but with the exception of those restrictions, they didn't care where the rest of the down payment came from. The contract holder had about $3,000 equity in the contract. We asked him to loan the buyer $1,000 on a personal note. He agreed and we closed the transaction.

In all, we had used four methods of financing—the first mortgage, the pledge from the seller, a commercial note obtained by the buyer and a personal note from the contract holder. Had we first secured the mortgage money, we probably would not have been able to hold the transaction together until the closing. The buyer would have become discouraged trying to borrow the $7,550 since we had difficulty borrowing the $3,275 we did get him. Quite honestly, we would have tried to get it all from one source had we known how much we needed from the start, and the lender would have questioned where that much money was coming from. It is unfortunate, but true, that if the circumstances had not been such to make it obvious, I might not have thought of breaking the loan up.

Another problem is that time makes the buyer lose interest. By having your secondary money arranged before he finds a property, or at least before you go to the loan application, you cut down on the time between the showing, approval and closing.

There are many secondary outlets that can and should be used to finance investment property. Since they are covered in the chapter on secondary financing, we will list them only for review.

1. Second mortgages
   a. Lenders
   b. Sellers
   c. Contract holders
2. Pledges
3. Commercial or private notes
4. Furnishings in buildings (installment)
5. Equity loans

CHECKLIST OF AVAILABLE AVENUES FOR FINANCING INVESTMENT PROPERTY

Something that few of us do, and all of us should do, is to use a checklist when looking for an avenue of financing. By doing this, you will not overlook possibilities for financing a property. It can be a very simple, but complete, list of all areas that might be used. Hopefully, this will keep you from finding yourself halfway back to the office and your buyers on their way home before you remember an avenue that would have worked.

1. Conventional
2. Blanket
3. Pledge
4. Equity
5. Contract
6. Notes

7. Higher offer covering closing costs
8. Second mortgage
9. Assumption
10. FHA
11. VA
12. Insured Conventional
13. Purchase money mortgage
14. Parents or relatives helping with one of above
15. Combination of any of the above

A similar list should be made for outlets available for these funds. It should include banks, savings and loans, mortgage companies, contract holders, sellers, relatives, credit unions, lease companies, federal government, insurance companies, finance companies and personal sources. Tape these lists on the inside of your listing book. You'll never be at a loss for a way to finance a property.

FHA AND VA — TWO FLEXIBLE AVENUES FOR FINANCING INVESTMENT PROPERTY

Outlets often overlooked, but extremely valuable when financing investment property, are FHA and VA, especially if the property involved is in reasonably good shape. The buyer must intend to live on the property and have plans for renting his present home. Once you have provided that answer, VA and FHA can solve many problems for you. Both agencies will finance up to four units and will allow the buyer to use the rental income when computing the buyer's ability to repay the loan. Requirements for FHA and VA and tips on how to use them to your benefit are included in Chapters Two, Three and Four.

CAPITALIZING ON THE INVESTMENT PROPERTY MARKET

In most areas, there is more investment property on the market than any other type of real estate. The reasons are simple. The owners get tired of collecting rent from tenants who won't pay, making repairs and paying utilities. The very nature of these properties puts several pieces of real estate on the market. People buy them to make money, so they are constantly wanting to sell them at a profit. The lenders won't give good loans on them, which means it takes a while to move one when it is put up for sale.

If you capitalize on this market, you will have an abundant source of merchandise to sell and buyers to buy. All you have to do is get them financed. It's not as hard as it sounds, if you use all the avenues you have available. You cannot take the attitude that the properties will finance themselves. You must anticipate problems going in, and decide on how you're going to solve them before you ever get to the bank. Try to get the owner to be present when the property is being shown as well as when it is being appraised. This is the opposite of what we've always been taught about selling real estate, but it makes sense in this case. Every time I show a building without the owner, the tenants either downgrade the property with complaints or hints, or they don't want to let us in. The owner's presence puts a stop to those problems. Tenants are concerned with having to move if the building is sold, and sometimes they are just envious of anyone getting what he wants. Do as much of the borrowing as possible without the buyer. In other words, make the arrangements and control the situation. A third party can always get something more easily and buyers have a way of not hurrying when they are handling any item on their own.

In each of the chapters on secondary financing and contracts, you will find information on how to use these methods to finance investment property. Combine these with an aggressive and confident attitude, and you'll finance properties more easily and more often than ever before.

CHAPTER SEVEN

Capitalizing on
New Approaches to
Conventional Financing

When you speak of conventional financing, many real estate agents think in terms of 80% first mortgages on a residential home, or whatever the bank will loan them on a given piece of property. Webster's New World Dictionary defines "conventional" as, "customary, or formal," but in real estate terms, conventional financing is just the opposite. Conventional financing need not be customary and is anything but formal.

Conventional financing is as unrestrictive, different and creative as the agents using it. To successful real estate salespeople, conventional financing does not mean 80% loans. It means *anything they need it to be.* Chapter Seven discusses different methods of conventional financing and offers examples of how you can shape it to serve any need you have.

OPENING THE DOORS WITH INGENUITY

To compete with your peers in the real estate industry, you have to have the ability to develop a financing program for each client that will reach your goal of closing the sale. The fact that banks are low on money, interest rates are high, your buyer doesn't have a large down payment, your buyer can't meet the normal payment requirements or that the home won't appraise high enough to allow you to secure an 80% loan is your problem and not your client's. Those reasons may all be valid, but they prevent your earning a commission. Your competitors are going to find a way to solve these problems, and so must *you*.

While conventional mortgages may not offer many of the advantages available through FHA and VA financing, they do offer one distinct advantage over government-insured or guaranteed mortgages. Conventional mortgages can be as flexible as your lender, and your lender need not be a bank, mortgage company or savings and loan. No government agency is looking over the lender's shoulder.

Realizing that they were not bound by government restrictions or red tape, many creative real estate agents have used conventional financing to develop programs in tight money times that met buyer needs so well that they have been adopted nationwide; for example, wraparound mortgages and FLIP mortgages. (These two methods will be discussed later in the chapter.) Your creative ideas do not have to have such a dramatic impact on our nation's lending policies to be effective; all they must do to be successful is fit the need of your particular client. Each transaction will be different; each buyer will require a different type of help. By keeping an open mind, and a creative and aggressive attitude, you can develop an effective conventional mortgage to meet your client's needs.

INSURED CONVENTIONAL MORTGAGES

First, let's take a look at insured mortgages and the conditions that must be present to use them. The two most common insured conventional mortgages are MGIC and AMI. They are insurers of conventional loans that permit lenders to loan up to 95% of the purchase price or appraised value of the home being financed. For convenience, we will refer to insured mortgages as MGIC loans.

There are two loans under this program: 90% and 95%. They have basically the same requirements; however, 95% will be stricter on the home and the buyer's qualifications. MGIC insures the amount of the mortgage over the 80% level. Anything between 80% and 90% would be a 90% MGIC and anything between 90% and 95% would be a 95% MGIC.

Many times salespeople forget that insured loans will work when the buyer has more than 5% or 10% down, but not 20%. You can use an MGIC with a buyer who has 15% down. It would just mean MGIC would only insure the top 5% of the loan. The purpose of these loans is to allow buyers to purchase a home without having to have a large down payment. The lender is assured of getting his money back in case of a default, thus allowing him to loan more than the 80% limit placed on most savings and loans.

Since a high percentage of value is being loaned, the lender and insurer will be more particular about the home being offered for security. It will have to be in a good location, in reasonably good condition and in a price range they feel is safe. There is a maximum amount that can be borrowed on these programs, depending on whom you are using. Most lenders also have a minimum amount they will loan.

The closing costs and interest rate on MGIC will be higher than on conventional mortgages that are uninsured. The interest rate will run ¼% higher and there is an insurance premium of ¼% on 90% loans and ½% on 95% loans. The closing costs on this type of financing will run one to two points higher than conventional, and about $50 higher on closing charges because of the application fee. The maturity on these loans will depend on the home itself for the most part, but can be up to 30 years.

MGIC is a relatively quick method of financing, compared to FHA and VA. They will take less than a week, in most cases, to issue an approval or rejection. The lender must first do his part by getting the employment and deposit verifications, credit check and appraisal of the property. In all, two weeks should be a reasonable period to expect for the processing. To qualify for the loan, the buyer should be earning four times the monthly payment as his monthly income after deduction of his total monthly installment loans. If a buyer now owns a trailer or home, he must sell it or have it paid down considerably and be able to rent it. MGIC requires that the buyer intend to occupy the home, and he is not allowed to borrow the down payment.

MGIC has its advantages and disadvantages, as have all methods of financing. It permits the buyer to get into a home with less money down than conventional, closing costs are less than FHA or

VA, and it's a much quicker process. It does not allow you the marginal buyer or property as FHA or VA does, however. When using MGIC, make sure you have your package together before going to the loan application. They will not permit too many things to be out of line. If your client's credit is slow, income weak, or the house in need of repair, you'd better switch to FHA, rather than lose a buyer because of a rejection. There are certain things that you can do to help the buyer with his down payment, such as gift letters, equity in an asset, etc., as long as it doesn't appear that the buyer is borrowing his down payment.

BLANKET MORTGAGES

A blanket mortgage is a loan that has more than one piece of real estate as security. There is no limit to the number of parcels of real estate that can be involved in a blanket mortgage. Normally, the terms on a blanket will be amortized monthly over a number of years with equal monthly payments. You can expect to get a maturity of 15 to 25 years, depending on the property encumbered. The idea of a blanket mortgage is to use equity in one property to finance another, without the need for two or three loans. If a property owner has a home that has a mortgage balance of $20,000 and a market value of $40,000, and he wishes to purchase a $60,000 home you have for sale, he can use the equity in his present home to buy the new one. You can secure a loan large enough to purchase the new property and pay off the old mortgage on the property he now owns. He now has $100,000 worth of real estate and a loan of $80,000. Both homes are on the mortgage as security.

The most common use for blanket mortgages is investment property, but they can be beneficial for other types of real estate selling. Assuming your buyer feels he can afford the payments for a short time, a blanket loan can allow him to find a suitable home, purchase it, and then put his present home up for sale. When the property is sold, the lender will reduce the mortgage by whatever amount they agree on to release the lien on the first home. Sometimes the borrower will want to put the entire proceeds from the sale towards reducing the mortgage. Others will only want to apply the minimum necessary to release the lien. When the mortgage is reduced by a considerable sum, the lender will also reduce the payments.

One problem you will encounter with blanket mortgages, is the borrower's unwillingness to give up the lower interest rate he enjoys on his present mortgage. There is a way to solve this problem and still arrange blanket financing. Most lenders will write the mortgage in a manner that allows the borrower to keep the present rate on the money he now owes and the going interest rate for the new money they loan, if they are requested to do so. Of course, you must be working with a lender who is in a position to do this, but, by using this method, you take away one of the biggest objections to blanket financing.

Blanket mortgages are the easiest way to finance 100% of the purchase price, and you can add to a blanket mortgage an unlimited number of times. As long as there is enough equity to cover the down payment on the property being purchased and keep the total loan within 80% of the value of all the property being used as security, the buyer can continually purchase property without a down payment. There is a disadvantage to using this method too often, however, in that the closing costs and points on the loan will be for all the properties and the total borrowed each time. This means the borrower's cost of obtaining financing could get very expensive. Remember when quoting closing costs, that each abstract will have to be continued every time a new mortgage is secured.

Blanket mortgages work particularly well when securing financing for new construction and purchasing bare ground, and can also be effective when financing commercial property. Anytime a buyer already owns a piece of real estate, blanket financing can make securing mortgage and down payment money an easy assignment.

OPEN END MORTGAGES

An open end mortgage is one that allows the borrower to increase the amount of the loan without rewriting the entire mortgage. The purpose of this type of financing is to get money on better terms for remodeling, built-in appliances, etc., so the borrower will have a lower monthly payment on these items. This method is often to the advantage of the lender, as well as the mortgagor, since it lessens the chance of the borrower getting overextended. An open end mortgage will not be of much use to you in getting mortgage money, but rather is a method of writing the mortgage when originated. The only essential reason to be familiar with it is to be able to recognize one when you see it.

If you have a client who already has an open end mortgage, you may find that it is also an excellent source of funds to purchase a home or to increase the amount of his present mortgage to release his equity and improve the terms on which he can offer to sell the home, since any additional funds borrowed on an open end are usually at the same rate of interest as the original loan.

BALLOON MORTGAGES

A balloon mortgage is one that has lower than usual monthly payments and has one large payment at the end of the term of the mortgage. The interest is paid out of the monthly payments, and at times some principal, and the remaining principal is paid at one time. This type of financing is usually found in construction loans, but can be of use in financing farms or residences. The most likely use to you as a salesperson might be to get a buyer a home of higher price than he can afford monthly. By using balloon payments, the monthly obligation of the borrower would be reduced to a level he could afford. In addition, you are going to have to show the lender a way for the borrower to pay the last big payment.

WRAPAROUND MORTGAGES

An interesting and important point about financing that most real estate salespeople don't realize is that new and more flexible financing methods are seldom if ever developed by lenders. Financing terms are initiated by real estate salespeople who have a particular client need to fulfill. You cannot survive by settling for the terms advertised by lenders; you have to develop new ways for them to meet the buying public's needs. Wraparound mortgages and FLIP mortgages are two such examples of real estate salespeople having developed programs that have been adopted as standard lending practices by most of the nation's lenders.

A wraparound mortgage is a mortgage that blankets or "wraps around" one or more other mortgages. For instance, if you have a client who has a first mortgage on a property for $30,000 and the buyer needs a mortgage of $50,000, the seller or lender can offer a mortgage that includes the first mortgage and the additional $20,000 needed, without loaning or paying off the $30,000.

Example:
Smith has a first mortgage of $30,000, a second mortgage of $15,000 and a third mortgage of $5,000. Each has a different interest rate and each is with a different lender. He has a buyer willing to pay $90,000 for his property with $20,000 down, but the buyer is unable

to obtain the additional $20,000 to assume the loans on the home. Instead of Smith giving the buyer a fourth mortgage for $20,000, he gives the buyer a wraparound mortgage for $70,000 which includes the balance on the first three mortgages and the additional $20,000 needed to complete the transaction. The buyer makes one payment, large enough to reduce his debt in the number of years agreed upon and to satisfy the first three lenders. Smith is still in the position of the fourth mortgagee and is responsible for making the payments on the first three mortgages.

The purpose of the wraparound mortgage is to make conventional financing more flexible, and its induction into your financing program gives you many added dimensions. The advantages of using this form of financing are:

1. The buyer is not assuming any of the mortgages. This means the lender cannot prohibit the owner from selling the property without paying off the mortgage.
2. It need not encompass all mortgages on the property.
3. The payment and down payment structure can be as flexible as your seller and buyer are willing to be.
4. The mortgagee will realize a greater return on his investment or equity, because he will be earning an interest rate equal to or greater than the rates on the first three mortgages. In essence, he will be getting a return on someone else's money as well as his own.
5. It avoids any prepayment penalty that may be charged a seller that pays off his mortgage before maturity.
6. It reduces refinancing costs, since the seller or lender is only lending the portion of the mortgage that is the difference between the purchase price and the total of all existing mortgages. If the wraparound is seller held, these closing costs offer as much as a 3 to 7% savings for the buyer.
7. You can offer the buyer, as well as the seller, many advantages. The buyer will most often be able to get a lower rate and will be able to obtain the mortgage with less down payment than if he were to secure the money in total from a bank or other lender.

The biggest selling point to a seller for using a wraparound mortgage is the return on his equity, compared with any other investments he might be able to make. The seller must also take into consideration that during tight money periods this method might be the only way he can attract a buyer.

The buyer, on the other hand, can save financing costs, enjoy a lower-than-market rate, get the property with less down payment and in many cases this may be the only financing method that will enable him to get the property he wants.

FLIP MORTGAGES
(GRADUATED PAYMENT MORTGAGES)

In today's market there are many versions of the Graduated Payment Mortgage (GPM). In fact, they have become a necessity because of the rising interest rates and costs of housing, compared to the rate of earnings increase. Credit for these programs and their success must go to the original successful concept of GPM called FLIP (Fleeting Loan Insurance Program). Designed by Allan Smith, real estate broker, FLIP has been accepted nationwide as a solution for buyers not being able to catch up with the rapidly increasing costs of buying a home. In fact, it is so successful that Smith receives a fee every time his plan is used by lenders and insurance companies anywhere.

What makes FLIP workable is the assumption that inflation will continue to rise, making the home worth more each year. Also, the buyer's income will increase, so even if he can't afford the monthly payments now, he will be able to within a period of two to ten years. Using the buyer's down payment of ten percent of the purchase price, the lender establishes an escrow account from which it draws a predetermined amount each month for a period of two to ten years and applies it toward the monthly payment on the mortgage. This allows the borrower to make a smaller monthly payment than he would normally be required to make and the lender still receives his normal interest and principal payment each month. That's what makes FLIP unique and acceptable. Nobody loses, since the lender receives his normal payment, and for the first few years the buyer has a reduced payment. By the time his escrow account has been depleted, his income has reached a level that enables him to handle the monthly payments.

Example:
The Johnsons purchase a home for $60,000 and have $6,000 to use for a down payment. They wish to secure a 25-year mortgage at 13% interest. On $54,000 their monthly payment for principal and

interest would be $609.04. By increasing the loan to almost 100% of the purchase price and using both the interest earned and principal placed in escrow, the FLIP mortgage would increase the original monthly payment to $670 per month, reduced by the escrow contribution over a five-year period to $570 per month. The amount withdrawn from the escrow account gradually decreases as the borrower's contribution gradually increases, until, at the end of five years the borrower is making the full $670 per month payment. By that time, however, his earnings have increased at a rate of 5 to 10% annually for a period of five years (which means he is now earning 27 to 54% more than when he purchased the home), and his home is now worth 30 to 60% more than when he purchased it five years earlier. Without FLIP, most buyers can never save enough down payment money or receive enough increases in earnings to catch up with the rising costs of a home or interest rates.

MAKING FLIP WORK FOR YOU

To make FLIP work for you, you must have a client who meets basically the same criteria that are needed for FHA Graduated Payment Mortgages. You will have to show that the home is one that will likely increase in value, and that the buyer has the type of position that assures him of annual increases in earnings of 5% or more.

FLIP will increase your sales, not only because it provides you with another financing avenue, but because it permits you to sell buyers more home than they can afford right now (which is what all buyers want). Every buyer likes the homes priced $5,000 to $8,000 over his head, and now you can sell one to him.

SEVEN WAYS TO BEAT A LOW APPRAISAL

If the buyer is short on money for closing costs, you can raise the purchase price in an amount equal to the funds needed and have the seller pay the buyer's costs. For instance, your buyer has enough money to make the down payment on a home he wants, but has nothing left for closing costs. The home is selling for $20,000. The costs to the buyer are going to be $500. Increase the sales price to $20,500 and let the sellers pay the closing expenses. This will work on either insured or uninsured mortgages. It is a very simple way to cover closing costs, but one often overlooked by salespeople in search of capital for the buyer.

We've all had the problem of a property not appraising high enough to carry the loan we need. Many people think this puts an end to the sale, but it does not have to mean a rejection if you look for the money you are short in some of the obvious places. There are several options available for you to pursue. Below is a list of some of the outlets you should check on before giving up on the transaction.

1. The buyer coming up with the additional amount required.
2. The seller reducing the selling price to the amount of the appraisal.
3. The seller pledging the difference, taking a second mortgage in that amount or a note from the buyer.
4. A contract holder, if any exits, accepting a reduced payoff or taking a note from the buyer, or seller or both.
5. Every party involved in the transaction sharing in the difference. The seller could reduce the home for his share, the buyer could put down his share, the broker could reduce his commission an amount equal to the other parties' shares, and the contract holder or second seller involved in the transaction could also contribute a share.
6. Change lenders in hope of getting a higher appraisal.
7. Any combination of the above.

CONSTRUCTION FINANCING

A builder with a good reputation won't have much difficulty getting construction money, but a builder new to the business or a private citizen might find it a little more difficult. There are few lending institutions that haven't lost money on construction loans. If the time is not right, the cost too high or the home isn't built well, the lender can be in trouble. They are aware of this so their standards will be strict for construction money. Having knowledge of what it takes to get construction financing can help you not only with builders, but also in selling bare ground.

The time to get in with a builder is when he is getting started. He needs someone to market his homes and help him get the money he needs. He needs someone to advise him on where to build and what type and price of home to erect. The salesperson he chooses will be the one who can help him now. It is, many times, easier to finance an individual building his own home than to get a loan for a builder who knows what he is doing. The lender knows that if a homeowner makes a mistake, he will live with it. If a builder makes a mistake, the home may not sell and if it doesn't sell, they don't get their money.

When working with a builder, the following information must be available for the lender to consider.

1. Experience of the builder
2. List of subcontractors to be used
3. Blueprints of home to be built
4. Costs of material to be used
5. Value of homes in area of building site
6. Value of site in comparison to value of structure being built
7. Proof that home is not only compatible with the value of homes in the area where it is being built, but also that it is in a price range that is selling well
8. Builder's financial and credit history
9. The anticipated profit of builder
10. Broker marketing the home

Having a broker handling the sale of the new home will make the lender more secure in the knowledge that the home will sell within a reasonable time. If you are having trouble getting your builder a construction loan, it could be that the lender is not convinced there is a market for the type and price home he is erecting. It might be time to use a little psychology and ask the lender what he thinks would sell well. Once he offers an opinion as to the type of home that should be built, he is on the way to approving the loan. Once the builder has proven himself, he can put up any type of house he wants.

The loan is usually issued in draws as bills are submitted to the lender. The loan will be written for six or twelve months, with a single payment when the property is sold or permanent takeout money is secured. If it is a "spec" home that is not to be paid off for some time, the note will be written allowing for semi-annual or annual interest payments. If it is a "spec" house being financed, be sure to tell the lender you will get as much of the permanent financing through him as possible for the homes sold from the model.

Sometimes it is necessary to sweeten the pot in order to get a commitment from a lender. Using the equity in the builder's residence as added security on the loan or giving the lender an interest in the project can increase your chances of getting the loan. More and more lenders are beginning to feel that they are taking all the risks on commercial and construction money, and if the project is successful, the borrower gets all the profits. For this reason, they feel they should have a "piece of the action" while their money is being used. It certainly gives them an incentive to make the loan.

You will probably not have too much trouble arranging a loan for an individual building his own home, if a few essential ingredients are present. While it is not necessary for him to be competent in all areas of building, he should have some knowledge of building. If he has lined up the right subcontractors and architect, he can act as his own general contractor. The loan will be written with no monthly payments for the first few months (usually six) and then regular monthly payments on an amortized schedule. The lender will issue the money on draws as the bills are turned in or in prearranged amounts at certain periods of construction. The builder/owner must show some equity, either in the form of cash or building site. Below is a list of information you should take with you for the loan application.

1. Credit of borrower
2. Equity of borrower
3. Financial status of borrower
4. Experience in building
5. Architect's drawing
6. List of subcontractors and cost
7. List of material and cost
8. Location and value of building site

You should take the borrower to a lender with whom he has dealt in the past, since your job will be easier if you are dealing with someone who knows the man is reliable.

FINANCING BARE LAND

Marketing and financing bare ground can be extremely difficult. Two factors contribute to this circumstance: the land does not produce an income, nor provide for shelter, until such time as a building is erected on it. If a building is going to be constructed in the near future, this problem will be solved, but if the land is being bought for an investment or a dream of a future home site, the buyer must be able to make the payments and pay the taxes out of his pocket. It is difficult to find buyers who not only can afford to do this, but want to. Not only is it more difficult to market than improved property, but since it doesn't have a building on it, the selling price is much less than improved property. Many offices will stay away from bare ground because of the difficulty in selling and financing this type of property. Anyone who becomes competent at financing bare land, however, will sell it.

As with any type of selling, you must take the right attitude towards this type of property. It has a very definite value and market. Without the land, there would be no buildings. You can add on to houses, build apartments to accommodate more people or tear down buildings and put up more, but there is only so much ground and everyone must use it, and wisely. Anything that has value can be borrowed on. The difficulty with bare land is that, because of being subjected to a limited buying market, lenders do not want to loan a high percentage of the value on the property.

Outside of cash, the first avenue to pursue is contracts. They can be written to pay out monthly or with small monthly payments and a balloon payment at the end of the contract. Contracts calling for the property to be paid off in three or five years with monthly payments amortized over a ten-year period and one large balloon payment at the end can be used to get the seller's money out more quickly and give the buyer time to arrange financing. We have bought several large pieces of acreage and divided them into building sites consisting of several acres each. To put attractive terms on the lots and make it possible for us to realize our profit before we were old and gray, we sold them on short-term contracts. The down payment was just enough to cover the commission and closing costs. The monthly payment was set low enough to make the land affordable, yet high enough to pay out the mortgage as quickly as possible. At the end of five years, the contracts were to be paid off. By that time, the buyers had established credit, paid in equity and the value had doubled on the land. This made it very easy to finance.

The second easiest method of financing bare land is blanket mortgages. Very few buyers of bare ground are looking at their first home. They have owned one or more and are now in a position to start thinking about building a new home. They can use the equity in their present home to get the financing they need to buy the lot they want for their future home site. Since the lot itself will usually not be that expensive, blanket financing can easily be arranged with the equity in their present home.

In conventional financing the buyer should be able to obtain at least 50% financing on bare ground. By using secondary financing, such as a note or second mortgage, you should be able to obtain a good portion of the balance. In the case of a builder, you can have the seller pass title free and clear and take a note for the purchase price. The builder can then get the necessary financing for the construction of a building. The seller can receive his money when the house is sold, which many times would be faster than waiting for a cash buyer.

MAKING THE BUYER AS DEPENDENT UPON YOU AS YOU ARE ON HIM

By now I'm sure you have figured out that the only conventional financing outlet I have left out is 80% residential loans. If your buyer is able to put 20% down and meet the monthly payments on the mortgage, your only problem is hanging on to him. Those types of buyers don't need you; anyone can show them through homes until they stumble across the one they want. You won't even have to attend the appointment for the application. Yes, he does need professional advice. Yes, you're more able to find him the home he wants with the least amount of effort. But are these factors going to stop him from leaving you if a for-sale-by-owner makes him a good offer or if another agent presents him with a house he really wants? Probably not.

What will keep your buyer in your corner regardless of the temptations presented him? The knowledge that when he does find a home, you have the means to solve whatever financing problems he has and get him into that dream house. He needs you, because nobody else can put him into that home, no matter how good an offer they make him. He needs *you*. You can create a financing program just for him. Who else can make him that offer? If you've done your job, nobody can!

CHAPTER EIGHT

Financing Farms —
Large and Small

Financing farms, like selling farms, requires an understanding of the unique individuals with whom you are dealing and their lifestyles. Not only are the buyers, sellers, and collateral unique, but lenders also use a different type of measure and talk a different language. For the average salesperson, farm financing is as difficult as commercial financing, if not more so, in that the rules of the game are completely different from those used to finance residential property. This chapter will show you how to think in the same terms as do farmers and farm lenders, and teach you how to overcome the many problems presented you when financing all sizes of farms.

DIFFERENT SIZE FARMS REQUIRE DIFFERENT TYPES OF FINANCING

Unfortunately, learning to finance farms is not as easy as going to lenders who lean toward farm loans. Unlike residential property, farms are unique in size, production capabilities, products produced, and value. The most difficult farm to finance and to sell is one that has an unusual amount of road frontage or abuts a residential area. Since the seller doesn't want to be cheated, he is likely to place a greater value on land that has potential for development than someone farming the land can earn from it. It is understandable that the seller doesn't want someone else cashing in on his good fortune, but this makes the property difficult to finance, since it won't earn enough to pay for itself. Your only solutions are to get a larger down payment from your buyer, arrange for a simultaneous closing on all or part of the frontage with another buyer willing to develop it, or get suitable contract terms on the frontage under a separate agreement. Forgetting this particular and unusual type of farm financing problem, let's take a look at the three basic types of farms and the best financing methods available for each.

THE THREE BASIC FARM TYPES AND SUCCESSFUL FINANCING TECHNIQUES FOR EACH

The first type is what would be considered a "gentleman's farm." This classification indicates property of under 80 acres in size. The owner cannot pay for the farm from the productivity of the ground. It provides more or less a hobby and a style of living. The second category includes the farm in the 80- to 120-acre range. This size farm will sustain itself, but that is about all. The owner must usually work elsewhere for a living and farm at night. The third size category can be considered the true farm. This is a full-time operation and requires a person who has complete knowledge of farming methods.

Because they are different types of operations, different methods must be used to finance them. They each present different problems with different solutions. The smaller farm is the most difficult, since the price is almost always high because of the demand, but the yield is not there to pay for the land. The middle-sized farm is not much easier since it barely pays for itself and the buyer must keep a full-time job besides. The larger farm is not difficult to finance if you are working with a true farmer; but if you're not, you are in for some work.

Financing farms depends on the ability of the buyer. The lenders know the land will produce a certain amount of income. They will be more concerned with the credit and knowledge of the buyer, since he is the one who will be working the farm. That is why experienced farmers can walk into almost any bank and get large sums of money for equipment, livestock or real estate. In other words, if you are dealing with an experienced farmer, you won't need this chapter. He can probably get better terms than you can. If you are not working with this type of buyer, however, here are a few things that will help in arranging the financing. On the next few pages we will take a look at the different types of farms and what can be done with each.

Type A: The Gentleman's Farm

The law of supply and demand says that the price on anything of value will be high as long as there is a bigger demand than a supply. That is also the case with the small farm. This farm is not likely to produce well and the buyer usually won't have the equipment necessary to farm what land he does have. The farm will not carry the payments, let alone equipment to farm with. The buyer will not be a farmer. If a farmer is ready to retire he is not going to buy a farm that requires the same attention that a big farm does without the income.

This means you have to find the right type of buyer for this kind of property. It must be someone with money or a good income, such as a doctor, lawyer, businessman or management personnel. The difficulty with most of this market is that the majority of these people would rather live in a fashionable neighborhood in town. I have found the most likely prospect to be one who has a smaller operation and wants to get a little more land, but does not want to go into farming full-time.

The easiest method of selling this type of property is, of course, contracts. The buyer does not have to qualify under conventional standards for the monthly payments and the down payment can be for any amount the buyer and seller agree to. The payments can be set up with small monthly payments and one large annual payment. The buyer can make the monthly payments from his income and the annual payment from the sale of his crops or livestock. The contract can be short-term or long-term. Later, the buyer can easily get a loan from a bank, once he has proven himself on contract. If there is any kind of assumable first mortgage on the property, every effort should be made to assume it; and you can use second mortgages or notes to get the down payment for the buyer.

Barring these two possibilities, you must turn to a lender. The size of the farm will make a difference as to which outlet you choose. If it is 50 acres or less, you will be looking at a conventional mortgage with monthly payments. If it is between 50 and 80 acres, you can search for conventional financing with semi-annual or annual payments. Savings and loans are a good source, but you can anticipate monthly payments for not more than 20 years and they will not count much income from the farm itself. Banks are the best source of money for farms in this category. They can be flexible in their payment requirements and smaller banks will loan a large percentage of the purchase price, if it does not exceed their lending limits to any one borrower. The Federal Land Bank and insurance companies don't consider this type of property a farm and will be of no use to you in securing financing.

A regular mortgage with a personal loan from a place such as production credit or a credit union is a good avenue to follow if the down payment is a problem. If you can get enough to reduce the amount needed on a first mortgage, the buyer will have lower payments for which to qualify. When the crops or livestock are sold, the buyer can pay off the note.

VA will finance farms, but the buyer must be able to qualify for the payments based solely on his income and not on the productivity of the farm. He is not only unable to use the farm income in qualifying, but must also sign a statement that he is purchasing the property as a residence and not as a source of income. There are two advantages to VA financing on this type of property. No down payment is required and the maturity can be up to 30 years. I have in the past financed the house and several acres on VA and the remaining acreage on contract. This reduces the amount of monthly payment required to qualify for the VA loan.

Excluding VA, contracts, assumptions and secondary financing such as notes or second mortgages, your buyer is going to need 25% of the purchase price down. He will also have to show some way to farm without going into debt for a lot of equipment. It could be that the seller is going to leave his equipment with the farm, the buyer has a source from whom to borrow equipment, or that the land will be contracted out on shares or cash rent. Cash rent works well because you can use it to prove to the bank that a certain amount of income is assured of being derived from the property.

When you list a property such as this, you should consider the financing possibilities that exist. Once you have decided what is available on a certain property, you have a better idea of what type of individual is most likely to buy it.

Type B: Self-Sustaining Farms

The buyers of farms in the 80- to 120-acre range won't be much easier to finance, but the property will. The buyer will not have to qualify for monthly payments, as the lender knows that this size farm must have semi-annual or annual payments that allow the farmer a chance to bring in the crops before making a payment. The lenders also know the land will pay for itself, if it is in the hands of a competent individual. The number of money outlets is increased, since we are now talking about farms. The problem is that unless the land is almost all tillable, you still won't attract the real farmer. You still have the problem of a large down payment being required and very few individuals on a farm this size have the equipment necessary to do all their own farming.

If your buyer has experience in farming, reasonable credit, and some equipment and equity in another property or cash, the Federal Land Bank is the best outlet available for farm loans. The Land Bank has two requirements: (1) They will only finance farmers on farms, and (2) they want to see experience and an operation that can pay for itself. If the buyer is not an experienced farmer, it may be necessary to arrange interim financing, such as a contract, until he can prove to the Land Bank that he can handle a farm.

If the owner is reluctant to tie up his equity in a contract, write the agreement with a clause calling for an attempt to arrange suitable financing at the end of one year and to continue this effort annually until financing has been secured. The Farmer's Home Administration can be helpful in raising the percentage of the purchase price that can be borrowed since they will work with the Land Bank on farm financing. In many instances, they can loan the remainder of the purchase price after the Land Bank has made a commitment as to what they will loan. Between the two, they will take equipment and real estate as security to enable them to loan up to 100% of the purchase price. Normally, the Land Bank can loan up to 85% of the value for a period of 35 years. The interest rate will float with the prime rate or cost of money. The Farmer's Home Administration will then loan up to the remainder of the value and take a lien on equipment as well as real estate. Since they work with the Federal Land

Bank, that's where the initial contact should be made.

Farmer's Home will loan their money at a lesser rate than the Federal Land Bank and not necessarily for the same number of years. Credit organizations designed especially for farmers, such as Production Credit, will loan money on equipment, crops, livestock or signature. We have used them many times to pick up down payment money. If possible, it is best to include the equipment in the purchase price, so better financing terms can be arranged. While real estate may carry only an 80% or 85% loan, equipment will carry almost 100% of its value. If the price of the equipment is reasonable, it can increase the borrowing power of the buyer.

Type C: Income-Producing Farms

When you get into large farms, the selling gets easier. The biggest problem is getting the listing. Farms are always in demand, and because of the value of large acreage, contract terms are often available. The seller usually cannot afford to receive all of his money at one time. The Federal Land Bank is your best outlet, but you can use banks and insurance companies, also. Insurance companies, however, are not highly competitive in farm financing. They want to loan only 66% of the value, their rates are higher than anybody else's and the maturity they want makes the payments ridiculously high. Local banks will offer good terms, particularly if they are familiar with the borrower, most likely a qualified farmer. It is almost useless to try to finance a nonfarmer on this size transaction.

THE FARMER IS AS IMPORTANT AS THE FARM IS TO YOUR FINANCING SUCCESS

Obviously, in any real estate transaction you must have two ingredients: a saleable property and a buyer with the credentials you need for the transaction. Farm financing requires a buyer to have more than just credit, income or down payment. He must also be knowledgeable about farming. Farming has become a very complex business and one that requires a manager who is knowledgeable in the areas of planting, harvesting, weed control, and which crop to plant which year and in which field. It requires an individual who can predict which crop will be in demand six or seven months from now and who is willing to devote long, hard hours in the fields or barns to earn the yield it takes to survive and pay back the mortgage at the same time.

The lender will be investing $80,000 to $400,000 or more in your buyer's venture, and they have to know that he can control the success of his farm and their money. Lenders know land will produce 'x' amount of grain or support 'x' number of livestock, and they can reasonably predict the value of these yields to determine potential income, but only a good track record can demonstrate your client's ability to them. One bad year can wipe out a farmer, and it's a long year until the next harvest. Unlike making your house payment in hard times, a farmer cannot very well tighten his belt and make an $11,000 or $25,000 payment.

For good reason then, the lender will be as concerned about your buyer's credentials as those of the farm. Your first step should be to evaluate your client's farming know-how and strengthen any weakness he might have *before* making an application for a loan.

FEDERAL LAND BANK: YOUR FIRST STOP

The Federal Land Bank is a nongovernmental lender that makes loans at lower-than-market rates to its members. Your client need not be a member to make the loan application, but one of the conditions of the loan and part of the cost of the loan will be his becoming a member at closing.

The Federal Land Bank is for farms and farmers. While they do make loans for other situations, all of their loans are farm-related, including construction loans for the farm house, barns, storage bins or other shelters. The officer taking the application will normally also be the appraiser and will have an important say in the acceptance of the loan application.

The Federal Land Bank is by far the most aggressive and knowledgeable of all available lenders for farm financing. They will want to see land plats, crop records, soil analysis, drainage and irrigation charts, equipment inventory, and the history of your buyer. Be familiar with these items and be able to answer the lending officer's questions or provide him with the documentation he needs upon request.

USING THE RIGHT BANK TO SECURE LOANS

Different lenders have different lending policies and this is particularly true when financing farms. The best lender, of course, is the one most familiar with your buyer and/or seller. Farmers and lenders have worked closely together for years and they have stronger ties than you do with the lender; but even so, they will often need your assistance to put the transaction together and get final approval.

If your buyer does not have a particular bank or if there is some reason his banker cannot handle the transaction, your selection should be based on the following criteria:

A lender . . .

1. who has a history of lending on the property.
2. who has a policy of making farm loans.
3. who is willing to give the buyer the terms he needs.
4. who will negotiate on the down payment required, taking equipment, crops and livestock into consideration.
5. who is familiar with the seller and one on whom the seller can assert influence.
6. who is the right size to handle your transaction. Don't take a 50-acre farm to an insurance company or a 500-acre farm to a small-town lender who can offer only a $100,000 mortgage.

FINANCING LARGE FARMS THROUGH INSURANCE COMPANIES

Insurance companies and pension funds are excellent sources for farm financing if your buyer is solid or if local lenders will not give you the funds you need. These avenues should not be considered a primary source, however, because of their lending policies. They are even more conservative than banks and their terms are for only the best of clients, or for the most desperate of clients.

Generally, they require 35% to 40% down and offer terms of only five to ten years before the borrower is required to refinance the farm. Getting the details about these lenders is very simple. Open your yellow pages to Insurance Companies or Investment Brokers, telephone all of the major companies and inquire as to whom you should call concerning a real estate loan. Chances are they will not have a lending officer in your community, but they will put you in touch with the officer nearest your city.

FINANCING SMALL FARMS WITH FHA OR VA

FHA, VA, and the Farmer's Home Administration offer good outlets for financing the small farm, particularly if your buyers are short on down payment funds. The requirements for these methods were given to you in earlier chapters and there are only a few minor differences for financing farms.

FHA and VA will finance farms, but will not allow the farm income to be included as income for the purpose of qualifying for the mortgage. This requires your buyer to have a very large income, but this problem can be avoided by using the method mentioned earlier in this chapter. By dividing the property into two plots, financing the home and a small amount of acreage and selling the remaining acres on contract, your buyer can easily qualify for the payments.

The Farmer's Home Administration will be easier to work with on farms, but they do present a different type of problem. Farmer's Home Administration will require accurate accounting of the farm's activity and of the budget of the borrower each year. This is not a problem for you in securing the loan, except that the information you provide will be more detailed, but it does have a negative effect on the buyer. This could mean future problems for you in dealing with the buyer.

CREATING FLEXIBILITY WITH CONTRACT FINANCING

Contract financing is used to finance farms more than any other type of property because of the large amounts of money involved. Not only would it be difficult in many cases to obtain loans at market rates conventionally, but also the seller often cannot afford to sell for cash because of the capital gains tax he would face. Contract terms add a flexibility to your financing that is often required to close the transaction. Because most sellers need to get their equity released as soon as possible, your job is to be as creative as possible to enable both buyer and seller to agree on suitable terms.

Conventional financing on a portion of the farm and contract financing on the remainder works well if the buyer doesn't have a large down payment. Since many sellers cannot afford to receive more than one-third of their equity in any one year, this method can solve both the buyer's and seller's problems and make the financing much easier for you to arrange. Short-term contracts with five-year payoffs or those that require the buyer to apply for financing annually also work well.

If the seller needs additional equity released, arrange for him to mortgage his property and let the buyer pay off the mortgage with his contract payments. In most cases this will relieve the seller of any liability for capital gains taxes and still provide him with the equity he wants to purchase something else.

By reviewing Chapter Nine, you can discover other ideas that will enable you to utilize contract financing to close the transaction, thereby earning you a commission check. There are no rules, no red tape. What you can do with contract financing on farms is limited only by your imagination.

SECONDARY FINANCING MARKETS

There are several secondary financing markets available to you when financing farms, and in the majority of your farm transactions it will be necessary to make use of at least one of these outlets. On many occasions you will have to combine more than one to raise the capital required. Seldom will you be blessed with a buyer who can put 25% to 30% down on a farm, so your efforts with secondary financing will determine the success of your closing.

Using both personal and farm assets as collateral, you should utilize the following sources when searching for secondary funds:

1. Production Credit Associations
2. Farmer's Home Administration
3. Federal Land Bank
4. Sellers
5. Credit Unions
6. Banks
7. Lease Companies
8. Private Individual Lenders

Before you get an offer on a farm, check out as many of these sources as possible, so you will know what is available when you locate a buyer. You also want to know their requirements in advance so you can ensure that you have properly prepared your buyer and application before presenting either. Get one commitment at a time when securing secondary mortgage funds. You can't wait for the entire loan to be committed by one outlet. You take what you can get and go to the next lender for the portion of the loan he is willing to make.

GAINING KNOWLEDGE OF FARMS TO IMPROVE YOUR FINANCING ABILITY

With any size farm, you have to know something about farming to sell or finance it. You must know what kind of income to expect the land to produce, the cost of equipment, the value of untillable as well as tillable ground, the problems of raising cattle and hogs, and the particular terms needed to allow the farmer to pay for the property. There are several ways to gain this knowledge, such as talking with lenders, reading farm material, talking with farmers and listening to farm reports. The best way to learn anything is to jump in and experience it, however. You may make a lot of mistakes, but you'll know what you did wrong and what you did right, and what will work next time.

CHAPTER NINE

Using Land Contracts and Loan Assumptions to Earn Quick Commissions

Every salesperson looks forward to receiving an offer with contract or assumption terms. Even with the new tighter restrictions on many loan assumptions, these two methods of financing are the easiest, quickest and most certain transactions to close, with the exception of cash transactions. By eliminating the appraisal alone, you have bypassed a major obstacle to loan closings.

Many salespeople, however, are closing their eyes to dozens of potential commission checks by not considering contract or assumption financing to solve financing problems at times when the buyer does not announce those terms as his only option. There are many ways to sell property to buyers using contracts and assumption, even though the circumstances might not immediately indicate these avenues are available. This chapter reveals the secrets of using contract and assumption financing to save sales and increase the number of quick, easy closings you can enjoy each year.

PUTTING LAND CONTRACTS IN THE PROPER PERSPECTIVE

Some salespeople have difficulty selling property on contract because they feel the caliber of property they deal with on contract sales is too low. "Contract" is a dirty word to them, so they don't spend the time they should developing this market. It is true that usually a contract sale will call for a buyer or property that cannot be financed. The basic misunderstanding salespeople seem to have is that this fact makes it difficult to close. They feel that finding a buyer who has poor credit with enough money to make a down payment is too difficult to be worthwhile. This is not necessarily true, however, since every property must have something going for it in order to sell. The home must be attractive, situated in a good location, be an excellent buy or have a feature that makes it attractive to a particular type of buyer. Many times that feature can be contract terms. Even if this is the only thing going for the property, you have a good chance of selling it.

A buyer, likewise, must have something in his favor. He need not have a large down payment or a good income, but he does need to have some good feature to make the transaction work. Most contract buyers realize they cannot be too choosy about the home they buy. They know they are limited on their selection and they usually have to reduce the requirements they set for the home they purchase. What a contract buyer has going for him is a desire to get into a home and a willingness to do what you feel it takes to sell him a home.

SELLING THE SELLER ON CONTRACT OR ASSUMPTION TERMS

The time to discuss contract or assumption terms is when you are getting the listing. If you wait until you have an offer in hand, you not only have to convince the seller of price, but also terms. You must begin putting the idea of selling on contract or assumption in his mind early in your relationship. The idea of an assumption is usually not difficult to sell to the seller. He receives his equity at the closing, as he would with a cash sale. Some sellers will balk when they discover that their name remains on the mortgage as well as any previous mortgagors on the same loan, and that they are still liable if the debt isn't paid. This fear is 99% unwarranted, since in most cases, the buyer puts down a fairly large sum to assume a mortgage. If for some reason the property does go into default, it would generally be to the seller's advantage, rather than disadvantage. He could then step back in and sell the property once more and make his money all over again.

If the seller has much equity, he will be protected against damage or back interest. The only time the seller is taking a chance is when he has very little equity in the property. Even with the chances of default increased as the buyer's equity is decreased, I have seen very few properties that have been assumed go into default. Normally, if the buyer has the credit to borrow the money necessary to assume the loan, or the income necessary to save his down payment, he is not the type of person who would allow his credit to be hurt by a foreclosure or allow his equity to be lost. If an emergency did occur that prevented him from making his payments, he would sell the property to save his equity.

If your seller will agree to an assumption, you have the advantage of advertising the property with an assumable loan. This adds another sales point to the home and should be pointed out to the seller as a reason for him to approve the idea of an assumption when you list the property.

Contract terms are harder to get the seller to agree to since his equity will not be released. All he will realize is whatever is left from the down payment after paying the selling commission and closing costs. The remainder of his equity will be paid monthly with interest. The type of home that requires contract terms will be obvious to you when you see one. If you are dealing with an owner of several houses or one who owes nothing on his property, you will have a better chance of getting contract terms accepted. If you are listing a home whose owner must use his equity to purchase another house, it will be more difficult to sell him on the idea of a contract.

There are several points you should make as to why the seller should consider a contract. The interest rate he receives is likely to be more than he could expect to earn if his money were in savings. The money will act as a supplement to his income and selling on contract could greatly reduce the amount of capital gains tax due from the sale of his property. These are all good reasons for selling a property on contract, but the best reason for selling on contract is that it is the only way some properties will sell. The seller has to decide whether he wants to be stuck with the home for the next 20 years or have an income for the next 20 years. A contract sale may not be the way he would prefer to market the property, but then, you cannot always correct his past mistakes. You can only show him the best way out of what he got himself into.

It is important when discussing contract terms with the seller, that you are not too critical of his property. It is necessary to explain to him why his home will not sell using conventional financing, but yet not to degrade the property to the point where you insult him. All too often you see salespeople who will go in and tear down a property in hopes of getting better terms or a lower price, only to anger the seller to the point where he would never do business with the agent.

Another problem is that you can never be too definite when telling the seller how his property will sell. You are dealing with many different types of buyers and sometimes you will get fooled. I've walked into homes and felt sure the owners would have to sell on contract because of the condition or location of the home. It was obvious that no lender would loan anything on the home and no one with money would be interested in purchasing it. Two days later a buyer would walk into the office and pay cash for the property. These sales always serve as a reminder that you cannot always put people or property in categories.

PROTECTING BOTH BUYER AND SELLER

A contract is an agreement between the buyer and seller for the transfer of real estate. The buyer does not receive title to the property until the conditions in the contract have been met. He does have a very definite interest in the property, that allows him to make use of the property in any manner he desires, within the terms of the contract. The buyer cannot place a second mortgage on the property or permit a lien to be filed against it.

The taxes remain in the name of the seller, who is recognized as the legal owner of the property. The seller is obligated to make payments on any mortgage that he has taken on the property. The seller usually has the right to inspect the property at reasonable times and the buyer has the right to make any payments on the seller's mortgage that becomes delinquent and to deduct this amount from the contract balance.

A contract should always be prepared by an attorney and recorded to give notice that the buyer has an interest in the property. It is also a good idea to have an escrow agent who will hold all the documents pertaining to the contract sale and collect the contract payments. This puts the abstract, deed and record of payment in the hands of a neutral party. If an escrow agent is not used, the buyer has no assurance the seller will transfer title when the terms of the contract are fulfilled. The escrow fee is usually split between the buyer and seller, since it is of benefit to both.

Recent state and federal rulings have increased the protection a buyer has on a contract purchase. It is now held that a contract buyer must not lose all his equity in the property, if it is more than what the damages and lost income to the seller would be. If a contract buyer defaults, the seller must not only give him adequate notice, but also must refund any equity over what is due the seller that the buyer might have given. This means a buyer cannot lose everything he has in a property. Not only will any money in excess of the down payment have to be returned, but also any principal paid by the buyer and the increase in value since he has owned the property. Only reasonable damages can be withheld from the buyer's equity. This is much fairer than the way a default has been handled in the past, even though it lessens the seller's hold on the buyer. Any seller who is honest should not mind having a contract under these conditions.

UNDERSTANDING THE MECHANICS OF A LAND CONTRACT

The most common reason for selling a property on contract is that the buyer or the real estate will not finance. The buyer and seller agree on a purchase price and contract terms. The expenses of the sale must come out of the down payment received by the seller. The contract payment is usually made monthly and includes principal, interest, taxes and insurance. The interest on this type of contract is usually computed semi-annually, since it is less complicated to figure than when computed monthly. This method of computing interest gives the seller a little more interest than monthly amortized interest would give him.

When it is necessary to have the interest computed monthly, rather than semi-annually, you can order an amortization schedule from one of several companies and give a copy to the buyer, seller and escrow agent. You will need to supply the company with the amount of monthly payment, interest rate, and number of years on the contract. An escrow agent is then chosen and all documents pertaining to the sale of the property are placed in the hands of the agent. Normally, the lender who holds a mortgage on the property will be the best place to go for an escrow account. The seller is allowed to place a mortgage on the property, but never is it to exceed the amount owed on the contract. As with a mortgage, the buyer is not permitted to allow or commit waste, except for normal wear and tear, nor is the buyer allowed to conduct any illegal activity. Many times, the buyer must obtain written permission from the seller before making any structural changes in the property.

In other words, a contract is normally used to sell residential property, with the contract being paid off over a period of years in equal monthly payments. The contract is written in such a manner as to protect the interests of both parties involved, and provides a means of getting people into a home when no other means exist. This is a very simple way of selling real estate. Now let's take a look at some of the more versatile and intersting ways a contract can be used to make a sale. Because a contract can be anything you want it to be, it offers endless opportunities.

USING CONTRACTS FOR 100% FINANCING

One of the most creative ways to use a contract is in obtaining 100% financing. Most banks and savings and loans will try to keep their mortgages at or under 80% of the purchase price or appraised value, whichever is less. Many times, you will have a property, particularly an investment property, that you feel is selling for less than appraised value. The appraiser will give you what you ask for, but that doesn't get you a 100% loan, since the lender will loan only 80% of the purchase price.

A man who already owns a property does not have this problem. If the appraisal will carry the loan, the borrower can have any amount he requests. If you have a buyer who does not want to invest any money in a property because of repairs he is going to make or just because he does not have any money, you can sell him the property on a short-term contract with no money down. He then can go immediately to a lender and, as the owner of the property, borrow enough to pay off the contract, or, if he is going to turn the property over, sell it quickly.

Either way, the seller can have all his money within a few months. The new owner can give any number of reasons for wanting to get a mortgage. He might be looking for better terms than the contract offers or might want to get the contract discounted by paying it off as soon as possible. Any reason that will make sense to a lender can be used. If for some reason the lender will not make the loan and you can find no one to do so, the buyer can return the property to the seller and lose nothing. The seller can be protected from losing any income by writing a clause in the contract making allowances for rents during this period.

The risk the seller takes is certainly worthwhile, since at most he will lose only a few weeks of selling time. Cover any problem you foresee by spelling it out in the contract.

Many times the borrower cannot get a good loan on the property, but the seller can. This could be because of the buyer's situation or the condition of the property. A lender would be more inclined to loan to a long-term owner of property, than to a new buyer who hasn't proven himself. Your seller can go to the lender, borrow as much as he will loan on the real estate and then sell it on contract to your buyer. He has released part of his equity and gotten someone to make the payments on the money he borrowed.

I once sold a mobile home and five acres using this method. The buyer had no money, except for $500 I was able to borrow for him, and his credit was less than average. With the characteristics the property offered, I knew it would take an excellent credit risk to get any kind of loan at all. I got the seller to agree to remortgage his property, using the proceeds for his selling expenses on this property and the down payment on the new home he was buying. The payments on the mortgage were covered by the contract payments and each party had what he wanted.

Even if the property involved is one that will not appraise well, the seller has a better chance of getting a reasonable loan on it. With a new buyer, a property that does not appraise well has little chance of getting any kind of commitment from the lender. By using this method of selling, the seller has not increased his liability much at all, since, if everything else failed, he could always rent the property for enough to make the payments if the buyer defaulted.

ELIMINATING THE CONTRACT MIDDLEMAN

Taking the first contract buyer out of the picture can be a problem. A person buys a home on contract because that is the only way the property will sell. If he gets ready to sell the home, his situation is worse than that of the person he bought it from; he cannot offer contract terms because he does not hold title. We've all had the problem of listing a home that has been sold on contract and trying to figure out how to finance it this time. If the equity is low enough, it may be a very simple matter to get the contract holder to agree to let your new buyer assume the contract. Nine times out of ten, however, it won't be that easy. Because of the value of the property going up in the seller's eyes, combined with the fact that he has been paying on the principal, the balance is usually too low for a buyer to assume. Your challenge is to find a way to bridge the gap between the selling price and the balance on the contract.

There are several ways this can be accomplished. The easiest way is to have the buyer give the seller a note for the cash he is short to assume the contract. The note cannot be tied to the property because the original contract seller still holds title and the property cannot be used as security by anyone else. This means the note would have to be of a personal nature with only a signature for security, unless the buyer had an asset that was free to use as collateral. The note could call for monthly payments or one lump sum payment to be made at an agreed upon date. Many times this cannot be done, because the seller needs his equity to purchase another home. Still, there is a chance that the seller taking the note might be able to sell it at a discount or use it as collateral for a loan.

Another way of taking the contract seller out of the picture is to go to the contract holder for help. If he is in a position to do so, he might be willing to buy out the original contract buyer and sell to your new buyer on contract, raising the contract balance to be in line with the sales price.

UTILIZING THE CONTRACT HOLDER TO SOLVE YOUR FINANCING PROBLEMS

We had a client who owned two properties in a poor neighborhood. They were both nice homes, but offered limited financing opportunities because of location. The smaller of the two had only a space heater, which made it practically impossible to finance. The owner was returning to the family farm he had just inherited and wanted to be rid of the properties completely. The larger of the two homes sold on the first day to a family friend on VA, but the smaller house sat for almost four months with no activity. Finally, the listing agent received an offer on contract from a young couple. The seller had purchased the property on contract, but we felt we could work something out, either through refinancing or assumption of the contract. The offer had just enough down to pay the commission and monthly payments of $90. The seller rejected the offer saying he did not want to sell on contract.

Two weeks later, I received an offer with less money down and monthly payments of $75 from a young couple who wanted to buy on contract and were very conservative about their monthly payment. They liked the home, and I felt they were the best prospects for it. Needless to say, I had to present my own offer, since the lister wasn't exactly overwhelmed with the idea. After I spent a few minutes getting acquainted with the sellers, I discovered that they really didn't have any opposition to a contract, they just needed their money. I got them to accept the offer subject to the contract holder buying out their interest.

The seller and I set up a meeting with the contract holder, who happened to be a friend of his. He agreed to purchase the seller's interest on two conditions. The seller's equity would be discounted to him and part of the settlement would be in the form of a note, payable in three equal annual installments. If at any time within that three-year period the new buyers defaulted, the amount remaining on the note would be canceled.

There is one problem you should be aware of when using this method. The person signing the offer and the person signing the contract are no longer the same. There is a brief period during which you are not protected for a commission and the buyers are not protected on any item on the offer. What happens if the person accepting the offer does not leave the drapes as agreed or give occupancy? Cover this problem in a separate agreement between the seller, contract holder, buyer and broker.

CONVERTING A CONTRACT INTO A FIRST MORTGAGE

The contract holder can help in another way. If he owes nothing on the property, he can change the contract with your seller into a first mortgage. When it becomes a first mortgage, title is passed. Once the original contract buyer has title, he can sell the home on contract to a new buyer. An attorney referred one of his clients to me who had just received all interest in a home as part of her divorce settlement. The property had been purchased on contract several years ago and she owed only a few thousand dollars on it now. The property was in a poor location and in terrible condition. The husband had been allowed to occupy the property until the divorce was final. When he moved out, he took everything but the furnace with him. I saw no way to sell the property on a conventional basis, but the owner was not in a position to finance the property so it could be sold on contract. We had the home listed for $9,000, which made it unrealistic for anyone to be expected to assume the contract balance of $4,000.

The contract holder owed nothing on the property and had been very satisfied with the payment record of the seller. I got him to agree to convert the contract into a first mortgage and to transfer title to my seller. An attorney prepared the mortgage papers and we could now offer the property with contract terms. This property could have been on the market for a long period of time waiting for a cash buyer. By using this method, the original contract holder's position was as secure as ever and the seller had an income to supplement her support.

If the contract holder does have a mortgage on the property, you still can work out an assumption. Let's say the property is selling for $35,000 and the seller owes $30,000 on the contract. The contract holder owes $25,000 on a first mortgage. The buyer is putting $3,000 down, which would leave the seller $2,000 after commission. The seller can take the $2,000 and assume the contract holder's mortgage of $25,000 and give the contract holder a second mortgage for the $3,000 difference. He then has title and can sell the home on contract to your buyer. By finding some way for the original contract buyer to receive title, you have opened the possibility of selling the property to a new buyer on contract.

USING CONTRACT FINANCING FOR COMMERCIAL TRANSACTIONS

On commercial property, contracts can be used to get the buyer in with little or no down payment. I have sold small corporations on contract by using the down payment to purchase one asset for the business and the contract balance for the remainder. By doing this, you have something available for the buyer to use as collateral so he might borrow his down payment. If the equipment is what the down payment buys, free and clear, you can go to a bank and get a chattel mortgage on the equipment, using the proceeds from the loan for the down payment. If the stock in the corporation was purchased with the down payment, the buyer can sell shares in the business, using the income for the down payment. If temporary funds are not available to your buyer so that he might purchase the business and then sell the stock, you can use your escrow account to hold the money until the purchase is completed.

I was once involved in a transaction that had the same problem. The corporation was an awning company and was selling for $90,000. This included the equipment, inventory, stock in the corporation and real estate. The sellers agreed to $10,000 in cash, contract for $60,000 and a note for the inventory in the amount of $20,000. The contract covered the real estate and the down payment bought the equipment and stock outright. It was a simple matter to sell the shares of stock to raise the down payment. The buyer had several associates willing to make an investment, so there was no problem with not being able to issue the stock until after the purchase was completed.

In order to protect the buyer and seller, you must use some common sense when putting a transaction together such as this. If you allow too much of the value of the business to be transferred free and clear, the buyer will have no difficulty raising the down payment, but the seller could be left with a large contract balance covering very few assets. If the buyer defaults on the contract, the seller could lose a bundle. You can solve any conflict occurring because of this if you are perceptive enough to foresee the problem.

As mentioned in the chapter on secondary financing, I once worked out a sale that called for the real estate to be sold on contract and the down payment to be used to purchase the equipment. We then borrowed the money needed for the down payment, using the equipment for collateral on a chattel mortgage.

HOW A SELLER CAN SELL ON CONTRACT AND STILL RELEASE HIS EQUITY

One of the hardest sales to work out on contract can be investment property. The seller may not see any advantage to selling his property on contract, since the income he is now receiving from the property is usually more than the contract payment would be. What he is generally looking for is to release his equity in the property. The only incentive a contract can give him is that he is out from under the responsibility of caring for the property, so the only way to bring him around is to put some dollars in his pocket. Most investment buyers do not have the kind of money it takes down to do this, since investment property lends itself more to someone getting started in the money market. Real estate is the easiest and quickest way for buyers to get a return on their money.

As with residences and businesses, the owner might be convinced to place a mortgage on the property, releasing their equity, and then sell the building on contract to your investment buyer. A short-term contract might be arranged to allow the buyer to acquire ownership and then mortgage the property to pay off the contract. If the appraisal is short and the entire contract cannot be paid off, the seller can take a second mortgage for the difference.

Another avenue you can take is to sell the building on contract and use the furniture, if any, as security for a loan, using the proceeds from the loan for the down payment. One thing that works well, when dealing with a seller who owns more than one property and is selling all or part of them, is to finance one or two of the buildings on a conventional or blanket mortgage, put the balance of the amount the buyer is short on down payment, and the purchase price of the last property on contract.

A circumstance once arose where two of my investment clients who were partners wanted to get out of the investment market and into construction. I called an investment buyer and told him I knew where he could pick up three buildings at a good price if he bought them as a package. He was willing to buy them if I could work out financing that required no down payment on his part. One of the buildings was a four-unit apartment building. Since this property had the most equity and the highest price, I arranged VA financing for it, subject to a blanket contract on the remaining properties. The contract called for a three-month payoff. The contract was for the entire purchase price of the other two properties. Once the contract was signed and the VA mortgage secured on the apartment building, the buyer made application for a blanket mortgage large enough to pay off the contract balance. Not until then did I receive the commission on the properties sold on contract.

The result was worth the short wait for both myself and the sellers. In less than two months, all the buildings were closed and the sellers had their equity. That was less time than it would have taken to market the properties individually. You can also put a higher or lower price on the buildings being financed. For instance, if the property being mortgaged is selling for $17,500 and the property being sold on a short-term contract is selling for $15,000, you could raise the price of the building being financed by $2,000 and lower the contract purchase by the same amount in order to put more of the equity up front and reduce the amount needed when the buyer refinances the investment. You could also reverse this principle and put a lower price on the property being financed to make it easier to get the mortgage needed.

When selling more than one property, there are many ways to obtain 100% financing. In fact, it is easier to get 100% financing when working with several parcels than it is when working with one property. When you are financing one property, you basically have only one price to work with and one value to depend on.

WHAT DO YOU DO WHEN THINGS ARE SLOW?

Real estate agents think they have to sell property to make money. When things slow down in the middle of winter, they pull in their belts. It shouldn't be this way. When my salespeople used to run into a slow spell, I would have them make money financing contract buyers. Not only did they make decent money from the fees for their efforts, but they also came into contact with people who were in the market to buy or sell.

We all know people who have sold property over the years on contract. Most of these people would rather have their equity if they could get it. If you ask, you will find that many of these sellers will pay you a reasonable fee to get the buyers off the contract and onto a mortgage. You then can approach the buyer about the advantages of having the contract paid off. It could be that the contract holder is willing to discount the contract, the fact that the buyers could have a tax exemption if on a mortgage, or that they would receive title to the property, thus increasing their borrowing power in the community. If they agree, the first place you should shop for money is the lender who holds the escrow account on the contract or the mortgagee who holds the lien. The lender acting as the escrow agent has a record of how the buyers have made their payments. The mortgagee on the property would be happy to consider a chance to get rid of a low interest rate loan with a small balance in trade for a new mortgage with a higher rate of interest.

If you don't know many contract sellers, there are several ways to find them. Lenders, attorneys, and the courthouse can all provide you with names of people holding contracts. This activity also produces leads, besides making you a few dollars for arranging the financing. Anytime you talk to that many home owners, it is impossible not to find somebody who wants to buy or sell a home.

ASSUMPTIONS

Assumptions are the easiest method of selling real estate, except for cash, and an assumption is a lot easier to work out than finding a buyer with cash. A buyer finds a home he likes, puts down the difference between the selling price and the mortgage balance, and moves in. You seldom need an approval from the mortgagee and there is no need for an appraisal. There are other ways to use this attractive avenue of selling, besides when your buyer has a lot of money.

One avenue to pursue to get assumption terms for the buyer is to have the seller remortgage his property for as much as possible and allow the buyer to assume the loan. This is a good idea, if the seller needs something to make his property competitive with other homes in the area.

If your buyer is short of funds to assume a mortgage, the seller can take a second mortgage for the difference. A seller can release part of his equity this way and have a monthly income at the same time. Many times the seller will not be in a position to do this, but you can use the same principle by borrowing from a finance company or other money outlet.

The same idea can be put to use to secure 100% financing. Let's assume your buyer has good credit, but no money. He could assume the seller's mortgage, give the seller a second mortgage for the difference in the selling price and the amount of the mortgage, and then go to a lender for a new first mortgage. If he gets a high enough appraisal, the new mortgage will pay off the first and second mortgage on the property. If you don't get an appraisal high enough to carry that much of a loan, the seller can reduce his second mortgage by whatever amount the loan exceeds the first mortgage being paid off. If you are fortunate enough to have a seller who can afford to wait a few weeks for his money, this method will be very effective.

ASSUMING BUSINESS LIABILITIES AND ASSETS TO REDUCE CAPITAL REQUIREMENTS

Many times when a business is being sold, a good portion of the seller's equity will be used to pay off accounts payable. You can decrease the amount the buyer must put down on a business by allowing him to assume these obligations. Not only the mortgage, but also lease payments on equipment, advertising contracts, utilities, and miscellaneous expenses could be assumed. If there is a good cash flow or hefty accounts receivable, this could work well for both parties.

Creating Commissions with Assumption Financing

You may have a client who has poor credit, new employment or some other problem that prevents him from getting a conventional loan. The property you are working with may require conventional financing and your seller is not willing to remortgage the property. What can you do? Not much, but one avenue you can pursue is to ask the buyer if he knows anyone who might be willing to secure a mortgage on the property and then allow him to assume it. Granted, this won't often be possible, but you won't know until you have asked.

FHA and VA can help when you are involved with a home that

is in a lower price range, bad area, or has a characteristic that makes it difficult to finance conventionally. If the property is such that you feel it will qualify for an FHA or VA loan, have the seller apply for an FHA or VA mortgage. Of course, the applicant would have to be a veteran to use VA financing, but anyone can refinance his home on FHA if he qualifies for the payments and credit standards. Once the seller has acquired a new mortgage on his home through one of these methods, he can sell it with little or no money down by letting the buyer assume his loan. This will give him the money to purchase a new home and put such attractive terms on his present home that it will be easy to sell. The seller gets his money on these methods from the financing, rather than from the selling of the property. This means you must make sure you collect a commission when he has his money, because with such terms, he won't need you to sell his house.

Assuming a blanket mortgage is difficult but not impossible. If the mortgage is paid down to less than the value of the property being sold, you can get the lender to release the lien on the property or properties being retained, thereby allowing your buyer to purchase the home on assumption.

Many things can be done with assumptions, but if it takes more than the seller's approval, there will have to be an important ingredient present: motive. If you know the seller's motive for putting his property on the market, you will know what can be done to put more attractive terms on the home.

CHAPTER TEN

Finding
Down Payment Money
Through Secondary Markets

The idea that all buyers have their down payment and that your only problem is finding them a home is true only in story books. If *all* buyers you deal with have *all* their down payment money, you aren't selling very many properties. It seems to be more and more difficult to find buyers with the money they need to purchase the particular real estate they desire. FHA, 90% and 95% MGIC, and VA are all excellent means of financing buyers short of funds. Many times, however, the property that you are involved with or your buyer's circumstances do not allow this type of low down payment financing. It then becomes necessary for the real estate salesperson to turn to secondary financing.

You must be aware of the different avenues available for secondary financing, where you can locate these funds, and which method is best for the transaction you are currently working on.

This is not always easy. Reading the problem is half the battle. If you are wrong, you could lose the sale. If you take too long to come up with the right answer, your clients could lose interest. Once you are knowledgeable in secondary financing, you will spend less time spinning your wheels and more time selling real estate.

USING SECONDARY FINANCING METHODS IS ESSENTIAL TO SUCCESSFUL FINANCING

There is a fine line dividing many of the secondary financing methods. It might seem, for instance, that second mortgages and pledges are similar and serve the same purpose. This is not true at all. Second mortgages require a separate monthly payment from the buyer, while the payments on a pledge are included in the first mortgage payment. Some lending institutions will not allow you to place a second mortgage on a property they are loaning first mortgage money on, while many lenders cannot accept a pledge because of their charters.

The seller's circumstances may very well dictate which avenue you use. Each method of secondary financing has its own peculiarities and specific qualifications. Knowing which finance company to go to with your client's credentials can save you time and maybe even the closing. Many times being wrong can be corrected, but in some cases, not being right the first time can mean the ball game. Finance companies will report to the credit bureau any rejection they make of an applicant after having run a credit check on him. If it shows up on your buyer's credit report that a finance company has turned him down, other finance companies might become gun-shy about loaning him money. This could mean an end to your transaction if it is necessary to obtain a personal loan or second mortgage from a loan company to complete it.

This is a good point to remember in any financing you do, but especially in secondary financing. It can be hazardous not to be right the first time. This doesn't mean you won't get the loan if it is not approved by the first lender you approach, but it does mean that you can lose ground if you don't know what you're doing. The manner in which you present the application for a first or second mortgage can determine the outcome of that application. Telling the lender too little or too much can jeopardize your chances of approval. Putting the package together properly takes great care and knowledge to ensure that you have covered all the bases and that you don't contradict yourself along the way.

Secondary financing requires imagination, persistence and knowledge. Every transaction you work on will have a different set of circumstances to deal with. The buyer's credit, monthly income, price range, location, and condition of property, current policies of the lenders, or availability of money are never the same. Because of the variations that exist, you must constantly be exploring new approaches to financing. No one can ever teach you everything available. All I can hope to do is to teach you enough about what has been done and what conditions need to be present to use a certain method so that you can get your creative juices flowing and relate these plans to the properties and people you are working with. As you read this chapter, think about how one of these methods might have been used to make a sale you were working on. Relate the examples given to similar transactions you are now working on. Use the basic principles given and relate them to your everyday business. You can't wait for the exact circumstances to present themselves as I have given them. It won't happen.

KNOW THE POLICIES OF BOTH THE PRIMARY AND SECONDARY LENDERS

Equally important is knowing the policies of the lending institutions you are dealing with, and what is necessary to remain within the guidelines they set. If they like to see a certain amount invested in the property by the borrower, make sure your application reflects that. If they disapprove of second mortgages, don't take them an offer showing a second mortgage on it. If you know one prefers equity loans and that's the lender you want to deal with, use that type of secondary financing instead of one you might have originally chosen. Don't lie to the lender, but there's no need to volunteer too much information. If the lending officer doesn't ask if you are using a second mortgage or where your down payment is coming from, let it go at that.

Many lenders will not like the idea of 100% financing or even 80% financing if the situation calls for a normally lower percent loan. Your buyer may not have any money for a down payment, and you want and need to earn a commission. Not being able to change these facts, you must deal within them. You will sometimes have to finance all of the purchase price without letting the first mortgage lender know what you are doing. Too many times we try to take the easy way out by saying the buyer does not have enough with which to purchase a business or a home, and we start working with a different client. This doesn't get the buyer what he wants and certainly does not earn the salesperson a commission. The buyer's lack of funds is his problem, but it's also yours. You are the one who must sell real estate. He will probably not be a failure if he doesn't get a certain home, but if you can't find a way to finance him, you may very well be. You must adopt an attitude that makes you aware that the buyer's problems and your problems are the same, except you have the talent and knowledge to solve the problems. That's why a buyer needs you. If he has 20% or 30% down, he doesn't need you; anybody can sell him a home.

DISCOVERING YOUR CLIENT'S NEEDS

One of the most common objections you meet, when trying to find new prospects, is that they don't have any money. They would really love to buy a new home or start a business, but they just don't have enough money saved up. This may be the truth or it may be an easy way out. The best way to discover which is true is to be able to overcome the objection. When you are working with a buyer or seller, you expect objections. You have practiced all the answers to overcome these objections. You have your response down pat, no matter which objection they present you with. Why not be as prepared when they tell you it is not possible for them to come up with the down payment? If you know how to use secondary money, you can overcome their objection and find out if that is really the problem. If it's not, you are closer to finding out the real reason. However, if the reason they have not bought is not having enough down payment, you have solved their problem. When you set about finding a buyer for a new property you have listed, you know the biggest obstacle is going to be money. You have two solutions. Find yourself a list of people with money or be able to find money for the people. I've found the latter to be much easier and more likely.

COMMUNICATING WITH YOUR BUYERS

One of the first things I do when talking with a new client is to put him at ease. I inform him that I am aware that having the necessary capital to buy is everybody's problem, and that I can get him the property he wants if the down payment is his only problem. One mistake that many salespeople make is to assume that the buyer has down payment money. We decide that a buyer of a certain price range, stature or income bracket will have his down payment or he wouldn't be looking. We indicate to our clients by our actions that we believe there is no problem with the down payment. Once the buyer gets this indication from us, he will not tell us if he doesn't have any money. It would be too embarrassing for him to admit that he is not as well off as we think him to be. He will either find fault with everything we show him or call another agent to sell him a home.

Don't put yourself or your client in this spot. Make him feel that it is normal not to have all the money he needs to buy a home. If you do not get the air cleared before too much ground is covered, you will have lost an opportunity to earn a commission. Time and time again, I've had a salesperson come to me with a difficult client, only to find that the agent had assumed the buyer had enough money when he in fact did not. In many cases it will take a seller willing to help with the financing. If this is true, you must know your buyer's needs before ever showing him a house. It would be an unhappy experience if you found a home the buyers fell in love with and you could not sell it to them because the seller was not in a position to help with the financing.

The buyer's desire to get what he really wants and a willingness to do what is necessary to get it are essential. If you have a buyer who wants the moon and is not willing to extend himself to get what he wants, you will be batting your head against a wall. He can't have his cake and eat it, too. I make sure buyers understand this as early as possible. I can get them anything they want if they can qualify for payments, remain within the restrictions I give them and if they are willing to put forth the effort that I decide is needed to get them the property. Where there is a will, there is a way. Unfortunately, the will dies out, in many cases, before the way is discovered. Two things can be done to solve this problem. Improve your strategies for finding the way the first time and make sure your clients are aware of what you are doing and that it's worth their wait to get what they want.

DEFINING YOUR CLIENT'S PROBLEM

Defining your client's problem should be the first area you tackle. We sometimes read something into a situation that is not there, or fail to read something that is. Reading the problem is not as easy as it might seem. The answer may not always be obvious. Many times the agent will overlook the answer because he or she is stuck in a rut. They get an idea stuck in their heads about how to solve the problem and they continue to pursue this avenue when it may be a dead end. I've found talking over the problem with an associate to be of benefit. Ask someone else who has not already made up his mind how it should be handled. They may have a refreshing approach that can solve your problem. I've seen too many salespeople decide that a certain avenue was necessary and that their client did not qualify, so they gave up. You don't know whether something will work until you try it. If a certain method is indicated, try it. Your client deserves the opportunity and you may be surprised at the outcome. Don't shy away because you think something won't work.

DISCOVERING WHAT'S AVAILABLE IN THE SECONDARY MARKETS

Knowledge of what is available in secondary money markets can be useful to you when dealing with contract buyers or buyers under insured programs. We all know that these types of financing do not permit second mortgages and in the case of insured mortgages, the buyers are not allowed to borrow their down payment or closing costs. If the buyer, on his own, acquires his down payment by borrowing it, it certainly isn't your fault. The problem that we all run into on contract sales is that the buyers usually do not have enough money down to cover the cost of our commission, the legal fees, and to put enough money in the seller's pocket to satisfy him. The majority of the time we must go out and borrow money for the buyer to use as a down payment. It is more difficult in some respects to borrow money for this purpose, because you can't use the property for security. You must use some other security or asset the buyer has to obtain the loan. On the other hand, nobody cares if the buyer borrows his down payment when buying on contract, so you are free to use any means to obtain the funds.

I once used a man's two horses and his eight-year-old sedan as security so that we could borrow enough money for his down payment. I have also found that a good way to raise capital for a down payment on a business is to sell stock in the corporation. The funds must be held in escrow until the purchase is completed so the stock can be issued, but it is an excellent way to raise a large sum for the purchase of a business. Anything is possible when using secondary financing if you can be original.

There are thousands of places to turn in search of secondary money and dozens of methods to use. These avenues are not limited to the four or five lenders on the next block with whom you do business every day. They include all the local banks, savings and loans, mortgage companies, finance companies, credit unions, as well as lending institutions in different parts of the state or different states, lease companies that purchase equipment and lease it back, commercial banks, and private individuals who have Certificates of Deposit, stocks, bonds, savings accounts, cash or a good cash flow. There is always someone willing to make the loan you need if you are imaginative and persistent enough to find him. You might put a package together that looks good to you, only to have it turned down by the lender you choose. That doesn't mean it was not a good idea or that it won't work. It only means that you have to continue searching for the right lender. It is not unusual for a salesperson to get four or five negative responses before he finds a lender who likes the looks of the package and will agree to make the loan.

There are several reasons for this. Lenders run short of mortgage money at different times and they won't tell you they are short. Normally, rather than admit they are short of funds, they will find fault with the applications they receive. Remember, you are always dealing with personalities when doing business with lending officers. They may be in a bad mood or maybe they don't like a particular type of financing you are working on. Each lender has policies that are a little bit different. Persistence pays off, however. After getting nine rejections, you might find a lender who has just received several large deposits or two or three loan payoffs. They have to get this money back into circulation and will loosen their requirements for a short time.

You should also learn something from each rejection. You learn more from your mistakes than from your successes. If you get turned down because of a certain point on the application, change it before submitting it to a different lender. You will at the same time learn the lender's policies on a certain type of property or loan. Next time you'll know immediately where to take a loan similar to the one you're now working on.

BEING PREPARED TO USE SECONDARY FINANCING

You wouldn't think of showing a house without an offer to purchase and a working knowledge of how to show the property, how to counter objections and a complete list of information on the home. You are prepared to write the offer right there if the client indicates he wants the property. That's good business. Why, then, will so many salespeople go to the showing without knowing what type of financing is available on the home? Financing is as much a sales tool as anything else. If you have to check with the sales manager or bank as to what can be done in the buyer's situation, you will lose the sale more times than not. The buyer has an opportunity to cool off, or some other agent may sell the house while you're checking. Know what can be done in any situation or at least have enough confidence in your ability to finance that you can talk intelligently to the buyer. If you don't have confidence in your financing ability, your clients won't either. And if they don't, they may start wondering if you are competent enough to handle their purchase properly.

When a buyer asks me about monthly payments, down payment, or terms available, I know I have a sale. I use the answers to his questions as closing points, and begin writing the offer. If you can show people how to get something on terms that fit their needs, you'll have no problem selling real estate. I'd buy anything if the terms were right—boats, cars, planes, pools—anything. That is an advantage we have over most industries. No other business has so many avenues available to finance the sale of its product. It is actually easier to sell a man with poor credit a house than a car. These people are easy to sell. They know they are limited and probably feel they can't buy a house at all. They won't be too selective about the home they buy if you can show them how they can get into one. This is a market that can be very lucrative for you. Most salespeople feel that people with bankruptcies, collections, low incomes, or criminal records cannot buy a home. They have rejected these buyers. Anyone who is willing to help them get a home will have a dedicated client and a source for sales that is virtually free from competition.

On the following pages I will give you several methods that can be used to obtain secondary financing. I have included examples of some of these methods to show you how to decide which is the best avenue to travel when securing secondary money.

PLEDGES

A pledge is a method of increasing the percentage of loan that the lender will agree to by using money from the seller. If the lending institution will agree to loan $40,000, for instance, and you need a loan of $41,000, the seller can leave $1,000 on deposit with the lender as a pledge that the money loaned is secure and will be repaid. The lender will then loan the additional $1,000 against the deposit made by the seller. Normally, 80% of the appraised value or 80% of the purchase price, whichever is less, is all that can be loaned. By using a pledge as security, the lending institution can increase its percentage of loan as much as it wants.

The seller must leave this money on deposit with the lender until the total amount of the pledge has been repaid by the borrower. Usually, all the principal paid on the mortgage is applied to the pledge until it is paid in full. The seller can deposit the money being used for the pledge in Certificates of Deposit, pass book savings, or any type of savings account the lender has available. He will receive the current interest rate being paid on the account he chooses to place his money in. He does not receive the same rate of interest the lender receives on the money loaned out. That is one reason lenders agree so readily to pledges. They loan money out at 11½% interest and pay the seller 7% or less on the money he deposited to make the loan possible. They have made 4½% interest without involving any risk to the lender on the extra money loaned. If for some reason the buyer defaults on the loan, the seller loses his money placed on deposit for the pledge if the default occurs prior to the release of the pledge. The seller has no recourse in the collection of these lost funds, as he might with a second mortgage.

I have always found pledges to be a very safe avenue for the seller. If the first mortgage lender feels his money is safe, the seller should feel secure in pledging a portion of his proceeds. If the seller is going to have money left after the sale that will be deposited anyway, a pledge can be a good way for him to sell his home. You can give the seller a reasonably close idea of when to expect the release of his funds by using the loan progress chart in the back of most mortgage guides. It will tell you how much equity is paid into the mortgage each year.

There is another type of pledge available to you. Many times the seller will not be in a position or will not have the desire to make a pledge for your buyer. Anyone may place a Certificate of Deposit or asset at the disposal of the buyer. If your client's parents have money in a CD or savings account that they are not willing to withdraw for the use of your buyer because of the loss of interest, they can sign a pledge agreement and allow their asset to be used for security. They can still collect the interest or dividend and help your client at the same time. You can use stocks, bonds, CD's, savings accounts, or any quick asset someone has; it can be someone close to your client or someone who is not involved at all. Lenders do not care who pledges the money or security, as long as they are protected. Ask your buyer about parents, grandparents, aunts, uncles, brothers, sisters, in-laws, employers, or anyone who might be willing to help him secure the additional money he needs without taking it out of pocket. As with the other type of pledge, the depositor is not allowed to remove the security until the pledge amount has been paid out.

Usually, however, you will have to look towards savings and loans to use a pledge. Because of their charters, many banks are not permitted to accept a pledge as such. Some banks will use the principle of a pledge by loaning the additional money on a commercial note with the asset as security, using a wraparound mortgage to get one monthly payment instead of two. When considering a pledge, you should become familiar with the policies of all the institutions that offer this form of financing. Some lenders don't care if you get a pledge for the entire down payment, while others will try to keep the pledge amount to no more than 50% of the required down payment. How you present the application to them can determine the actual percentage of pledge they'll allow. If you know they require a matching amount of down payment with a pledge, find some way to ask for that. The circumstances might change later and you might have to go back and ask for a higher percentage of the pledge, but by then the lender would have had an opportunity to look over your buyer. Many times the lender will increase the limit on percentage of pledges, if they fail to appraise the property for the required figure.

USING PLEDGES FOR COMMERCIAL TRANSACTIONS

I once sold a laundromat to a buyer who had no money, but felt he could borrow $5,000 to use for down payment, closing costs, operating and opening expenses. I knew we had two problems right away. The lenders were not going to like the idea of a client with no money of his own invested, and $5,000 was not enough money down, let alone all the other purposes it had to serve. The purchase price was $35,000, which was an excellent buy. The price included all the equipment (fairly new), spare parts, inventory and the building. The building was in an excellent residential neighborhood, in good condition, offered an extra storeroom, and the lot was 365′ × 150′. The woman selling the business was in poor health and had shut the laundromat down.

These things were in our favor. The price was at least $15,000 less than what the property was worth, were it not a distress situation.

The seller was anxious to rid herself of the responsibility and would do whatever was needed to move the property. Working with a commerical property, we knew we could not expect more than a 75% loan on the real estate. We could, because of the condition and value of the equipment, get almost 100% financing on the equipment and the seller agreed to pledge $7,500 or take a second mortgage.

Here is where we had to take a long look at what we really needed and wanted. The savings and loans were the only places we could get a pledge, but they could not loan on the equipment. The local banks were eliminated for two reasons. One, they wouldn't take a pledge and by having to borrow the down payment, the buyer could not afford second mortgage payments; and two, the buyer was going to borrow his $5,000 from them and thus it would have been difficult to borrow the first mortgage money from them as well.

We had had considerable luck with a small bank in another community that was willing to enter our market. We decided to put the package together and take it to them. We asked for a $32,500 loan with the following conditions. The seller would leave $7,500 with the lender in the form of a CD. The bank would make a commercial loan to the buyer for that amount. A loan of $20,000 would be made on the real estate, and $5,000 would be loaned on the equipment using a chattel mortgage, with $2,500 of the money to be given to the buyer for operating capital. The buyer than put $5,000 down and we completed the purchase. The package mortgage payments would be higher for the first seven years. This was done so that the equipment would be paid out as it depreciated.

It's important to recognize two things with this sale. First, we had something going for us. There must be some element to work with. It need not be money or credit, but you have to have a good property, or a good buyer, or a willing seller, or good timing; something has to be on your side. Second, we decided what the problem was and went about solving it with the best method we had available. If we had approached one of the banks that the buyer was going to borrow his down payment from, we might have ruined his chance of getting the down payment money. By using a small bank we could impress upon them the good price at which the property was selling, and even though they were increasing the normal loan amount, they were protected.

I never stop selling. You have to sell the buyers, the sellers, the lenders, and even the appraisers. To be successful, you have to have the ability to get other people to see things your way.

Advantages of Using a Pledge

Most of the time you will be using pledges on residential property. There is an advantage to using a pledge over insured mortgages, such as MGIC. By using a pledge, you have reduced the amount of money required from your buyer as you would with a 90% or 95% loan, but you can get them a lower rate of interest on a conventional loan and they will have fewer closing costs to pay. The interest rate on an insured loan will run from ¼% to ½% higher because of the insurance on the mortgage charged by the insurer. The closing costs will run one to two points higher because the lender must share them with the insurer. MGIC puts a limit on how small or how large an amount they will loan. On a conventional loan with a pledge, you can sell houses in lower price ranges and in poorer condition. There will be times when you submit an application on MGIC and it's turned down because of the house. The seller now is willing to listen because the bank has told him what you've been trying to tell him since you listed his house. Switch to a pledge if the lender is agreeable to the idea. You can show the buyer how it will be better for him and you can show the seller why this may be the only way he can sell his home.

Why a pledge, instead of a second mortgage? As I pointed out earlier, many institutions do not like to have second mortgages placed on property they are loaning first mortgage money on. Your buyer may not be able to afford the extra payment that a second mortgage would require. By using a pledge, the buyer can borrow money on a second mortgage for repairs or any other reason he might wish. The seller does not have to worry about collecting payments and can draw his interest while his money is on deposit.

Both are good methods. There are times (most of the time) when only one of these avenues would work because of the circumstances you have to deal with. That is why you must be able to use both in selling real estate. It's not a matter of which is best, but rather which is necessary to make the offer work. Like it or not, if you can't finance it, you can't sell it.

SECOND MORTGAGES

A second mortgage is a junior lien on a piece of real estate. It gives the mortgagee a lien on the property as security for a loan. Everything that is necessary for a first mortgage to be legal is required for a second mortgage. The second mortgagee does have the right of foreclosure under the same regulations governing first mortgages, but it is necessary for the second mortgage holder to force the foreclosure of the first mortgage and then bid high enough at the sheriff's sale to protect his interest. All proceeds from the sale of a property at a sheriff's sale will first be applied towards the first mortgage, and any money left over will be applied to the second mortgage. If the property does not bring enough to clear the first mortgage holder out, the second mortgagee receives nothing. In other words, his money is protected, but only to a certain point and only if he knows how to protect himself. A second mortgage must be recorded to protect the mortgagee against the sale of the property without paying off the second mortgage.

The most common use for second mortgages is to reduce the amount of capital required from a buyer to purchase a piece of real estate. Usually the seller of the property will take a second mortgage as part of the purchase price. Instead of paying the money at the closing in cash, the buyer will sign a second mortgage and note and pay monthly installments to the seller with interest.

There are other means of securing second mortgage money, however, and many other purposes for second mortgages. Let's explore some of the situations that might require second mortgages, where to get the second mortgage loan, and how to use second mortgages to sell real estate.

Lending Institutions

Many times, the seller is unwilling or unable to accept a second mortgage. When this situation occurs, you must turn to a lender who is willing to loan secondary money. Normally savings and loans and many banks will not make second mortgage loans. This leaves your most likely possibility to be finance companies. They advertise second mortgage money and are very aggressive in their lending policies. Finance companies still like to see their loans within the 80% formula used by banks and savings and loans, minus the first mortgage. This means you have to do a little work to get them to loan you all the down payment money you need or a good portion of it.

One way to get the money you need from them is to get a higher appraisal than the purchase price calls for. If the property appraises out, they will be easier to deal with. The best way to get all the money you need is to include other assets that your buyer has as security for the loan. Many loan companies will loan second mortgage money and include autos, boats, furniture, or motorcycles as security.

The rates charged by finance companies are quite high as compared to those for first mortgage money. If the property you are working with offers a good income, very low rate of interest that's assumable, or your client intends to pay off the loan in a short period of time, a finance company is worthwhile to use. Its rates may be high, but it is a very good outlet to have available for second mortgage money.

Some banks will loan money on second mortgages. It may be necessary for your client to be a customer of theirs to obtain second mortgage money, however. There is a risk factor in second mortgages and for this reason, banks, being traditionally conservative, will stay away from them. The only way to find out how a bank feels about a second mortgage is to ask an officer. If you get a bank to commit itself to loaning second mortgage money, you have created a new outlet for secondary financing.

Credit unions are always good places to turn in search of second mortgage money. Their rates are lower and they are easier to deal with because they know they are going to get their money before anyone else, as long as the borrower works. Most of your larger companies have credit unions big enough to handle this type of loan.

A good source for secondary money is the newspaper and trade magazines. Companies that specialize in second mortgages will advertise for borrowers. They may be commercial companies or a private individual looking for a return on their money. We will discuss this avenue of securing secondary money next.

Private Individuals

You will run across a seller once in a while who financed his home through the previous owner or another individual. He may have given them a mortgage on the property and had title passed to him. If this situation occurs, you have a good outlet for second mortgage money. If the seller is unable to take a second mortgage, the obvious individual to turn to is the person holding the mortgage. He is not anticipating a payoff, he is probably still looking for a return on his money and he does not have strict guidelines that your buyer must stay within. You can show the mortgagee how to release a portion of his investment and get a better return on the remainder than he was realizing before. He still has a lien on the property, so his money is protected.

I once sold a motel for $100,000 for which the mortgagee was the former owner. My buyer had only a few thousand dollars to put down and there were two large chain motels under foreclosure within a mile of the one I had. There was a good reason for this situation. The motels were new and the construction cost had been better than $20,000 per unit. The volume of business had to be very large for them to be successful. The unit cost on my buyer's motel was less than $5,000, so the operator could afford to do less volume and at a lower rate. The banks couldn't quite see it my way though, and I was having a difficult time arranging the financing.

The former owner was living in Florida, which didn't help much as far as communication was concerned. I finally got a bank to agree to a $50,000 first mortgage loan. The seller was not willing to take more than $5,000 on a note. I called the mortgagee and asked him to trade his first mortgage of $50,000 for a second mortgage of $40,000 with a 3% higher interest rate than he was now receiving. After hearing my problem, he agreed to take $10,000 in cash, a second mortgage for $40,000 and release the first mortgage.

I could not have sold that motel to a man with $5,000 if the first mortgagee had not agreed to take a second mortgage. Some people think I'm just lucky, but I think I have success because I am always looking for that one ingredient that will make it work. It's there in almost every case; it's just a matter of finding it.

If you are dealing with a property that has been sold on contract, the contract seller might be willing to make your client a second mortgage loan. If he wants his money out, getting part of it is better than getting none, and if he doesn't want the contract paid off, he will be happy to make a second mortgage loan. Look for the most likely person to be of help. It does no good to sit around and stew because your seller is unable or unwilling to take a second mortgage. Find a person who *is* willing to make the second mortgage loan. Not asking the question has allowed more opportunities to slip by than anything else.

A second mortgage and note should always be prepared by an attorney. The attorney will ensure that all the necessary information is contained in the documents to make them legal and binding. Your only responsibility will be to inform him of the interest rate, term of loan, and method of repayment. These can all be very flexible on a second mortgage to fit your buyer's and seller's needs. A second mortgage can be drawn up requiring only interest payments until the maturity date, at which time the principal and any accrued interest would be due. You can even use an upcoming date or event as the maturity of the mortgage, remembering that all mortgages must allow for a final payoff date. It might be written like this:

This second mortgage shall be paid in full upon the inheritance of the mortgagor being received by same; however, the note will be due no later than July 1, 1989.

You might need to base the payoff of the note on a divorce decree, discharge from service, receipt of forthcoming proceeds, or dissolution of a business or partnership. Normally, your seller should be able to get ½% to 1% higher interest rate than the current first mortgage rate, on a second mortgage. This is a better return than the mortgagee could hope to obtain by depositing his funds in a savings account, yet reasonable enough that the buyer can afford to use this means of financing.

Second mortgages can also be obtained by the seller so that he might be able to sell the property on assumption or contract. A buyer may want to place a second mortgage on his present property and use the proceeds as a down payment on the new home he is purchasing. The advantage of this is that he could save the lower interest rate that he now enjoys on his present property and mortgage if he intends to keep his present property. In the case of buying an investment property, either the anticipated profit from a quick resale or the income from the property could make it worthwhile to use a second mortgage even if it required a higher rate of interest than the buyer may wish to pay.

As previously pointed out, second mortgage rates are usually high. If you are dealing with a property that offers a return, figure the interest on the second mortgage as an expense and if you still have a favorable return, it is wise to use this method.

HOW A SECOND MORTGAGE EARNED ME THREE COMMISSIONS

I once sold a restaurant to a woman with only $300 down. I got my first mortgage commitment and then went to the sellers for the balance. If it weren't for the second mortgage, I would not have sold the property. That was the first commission I earned.

The sellers then approached me a year later about turning their second mortgage into cash. I could not find anyone interested in purchasing the note because of the recent jump in interest rates, but we had an apartment building for sale that was owned by a woman who had several properties and was in poor health. She wanted to start liquidating her assets, so I got my client to agree to use the second mortgage he had taken on the restaurant to buy the apartment building. The seller agreed to sell the building for $15,000, taking the second mortgage as $6,000 of the purchase price. I then arranged a loan to cover the balance.

This did several things for the buyer and for the seller as well. The buyer had changed the second mortgage to a saleable asset with a larger monthly income than the second mortgage offered. The seller had gotten rid of a property she could no longer maintain, received enough cash to pay the property off and obtained an income without any effort involved from collecting. This was my second commission.

I listed the apartment building for sale again after some repairs were made and sold it for $2,000 more than the buyer had paid. Not only did I earn a few dollars for them but I turned the note they were holding into cash, which is what they originally wanted. This earned me my third commission.

All it takes is to look for the buyers and sellers who possess what the other needs. Many times we pass up commissions by not matching up our buyers and sellers. We don't sit down and ask ourselves, "What type of buyer or seller do I need to make this work?" Second mortgages are flexible enough in the payment method and buyer requirements that they can be made to work in almost any situation in which you need help. Just keep an open mind about how they can work for you. Be original. There's nothing wrong with being the first salesperson to try something. You don't have to know it will work to try it. In fact, you're probably better off if you are first. By the time anybody figures out what you are doing, you will have already closed the loan.

There is nothing wrong with third or fourth mortgages if you can find a party to take them. It might be that after getting the limit on a second mortgage, you still need more money. Look to a private individual for a third mortgage to obtain the balance you need. Never give up on obtaining the money you need; there are thousands of outlets across the country for money. Many times you can go out of your area to get a loan. Remember, if you give up at nine, the tenth one might be the lender who would say "yes." They all look at applications a little bit differently, and they all receive an unexpected increase in deposits or payoffs at certain times. There *is* money available somewhere for what you need, so find it.

NOTES

There are times when a pledge or second mortgage is either not possible, or not enough for your buyer's needs. When this happens, you quite obviously need to look elsewhere for money. Notes, either personal or commercial, should be the first place you look. Usually the buyer is not willing to sell an asset to get what he wants. However, he will often borrow the needed funds if you can show him the way. If borrowed at the right time or in the right manner, notes can be a profitable avenue. It is important that the timing or manner of borrowing is right because if the note shows up at the wrong time, the lender might refuse to make the loan. If possible, the money borrowed from a commercial source (one that will show up on a credit report) should be borrowed after loan approval or well in advance. Although the lender may not care if the buyer borrows the money needed, the debt might hurt his chances of qualifying for the loan. Some lenders may not care for the idea of 100% financing, even if they are not carrying all of it.

Commercial Notes

The best place to go for a commercial note is to a lending institution that has dealt with your client in the past and where he has established a good record. Sometimes security other than a signature will be required and other times it won't.

Credit unions are always good places to get a personal loan for a couple of reasons. They will be more likely to loan your client money without a hassle because they know they get their money before he gets his paycheck. The loan will usually not show up on the credit application and the interest rate charged by credit unions will be better than you could probably obtain elsewhere. If your client does not have an asset to use for collateral, a credit union will take co-signers for security.

If your buyer feels that he cannot afford an additional payment, he might go to his bank and receive a loan on a six-month note that he can pay when he gets an upcoming bonus, tax return, vacation pay, etc. To obtain this type of loan in a large enough amount to do you any good, your client will have had to have a good record with the bank involved or have a very good credit picture. If your buyer has an auto loan with a bank and some of it has been paid off, he may be able to refinance the car and use the additional money received for the purchase of his new home.

Finance companies are probably your best outlet for money on personal notes if the amount needed is not exorbitant. They don't make money on trust accounts or buying short-term government bonds. They are in the business of loaning money and are happy to do it if you have a halfway decent buyer.

With all commercial loans, the reason you give them for borrowing the money is important. If they are aware that it is for the purchase of real estate, they will either ask for a second mortgage or refuse to loan for that purpose. Have a good reason for borrowing the money. If your buyer has done enough business with the lender you choose, he probably will not have to explain why he wants the money and of course, if you should be lucky enough to have a buyer with assets in the form of Certificates of Deposit, stocks or savings bonds, you can borrow 100% on them without any question. If your client has someone close to him who has these assets that they are willing to use for security, you can also get a good term loan on them. One point for your side to remember is that when borrowing on this type of asset, you can get the lowest interest rate available for your client. Most times the rate of interest charged will not be much higher than the return realized by the asset used as security. The bank has no liability, so it is willing to receive less interest.

Private Notes

Don't forget private notes from individuals either involved in the transactions, close to the buyer or seller, or outside sources. If you have these available to you, it will be easier to obtain money from them than by going through commercial institutions. The lender can know why you are borrowing the money, is not as concerned about the borrower's credit, and will settle for less collateral. I have had sellers who were not willing to pay the buyer's closing costs, but were willing to take a note from the buyer for the closing costs and allow them to be paid out of the proceeds of the sale.

I once sold an apartment building that had been purchased on contract by the seller. He did not have enough equity to take a note for part of the down payment, so we went to the contract holder and convinced him to agree to loan the buyer the additional money needed. He received most of his equity in the contract, made the sale possible and still had a monthly income from the note.

Many times, Mom and Dad have loaned their children money to purchase a property until their present home was sold or just to help the buyer get the property. I personally have even taken a few notes from the buyer, using part of my commission. They provided me with a partial commission, a small monthly income and a few satisfied clients. There is nothing your clients like to see more than your personal belief in the people you're working with. If you are willing to take part of the liability, they are more willing to assume part of the liability. It would probably be better to receive the commission in cash, but part of a pie is better than none at all.

I had two investment buyers who wanted to build a good real estate portfolio, but did not want to invest any cash. I arranged for the purchase of a property with the seller taking a note for the total down payment. The bank was not concerned because no second mortgage was involved, and the note was to be paid when the buyers sold their cattle. This gave the bank a definite method of repaying the note and an asset detached from the real estate for security. As far as the bank was concerned, the buyers were putting something into the property by using an asset. I think the cattle died before the note was paid, but our intentions were never questioned, and the seller and buyers were all happy. Banks will usually not mind personal notes between the buyer and seller even for the total amount of the down payment if the note is tied to a definite event or asset.

In addition, insurance companies will loan money on the cash value of life insurance policies. Many buyers don't know what assets they have to borrow against or raise money with until you ask. They'll tell you they don't have anything available, but when you start down the list, they soon discover they do have methods of obtaining money. That's why it's important that you don't give up when the buyer says he can't raise the money to buy a home. Show him how it can be done. Everyone has some way to obtain money.

I was once referred to an elderly school teacher by our minister. She had no cash, but did have a reasonable income. It was very hard to pin down what she had available for a down payment; however, I did know that to ensure a sale, I was going to have to find a home on an assumption, because of her age. I did find such a home in a perfect location near my client's school. She would need only $3,000 to assume the loan. It was not until the offer was written that she finally admitted she had no funds and no method of obtaining the down payment except for the sale of some Teacher's Association bonds that she owned. She agreed to sell them and we wrote the offer.

The problem developed when she was unable to market the bonds. They were not cashable for several years and there were no buyers for them. I talked to a local banker in the commercial loan department, and he agreed to loan my buyer the needed money, using the bonds as security. If I had taken my client's word that she had no assets to use to purchase a home, I would not have earned a commission. People don't lie to you about what they don't have; they just do not know what you can do with something that they take for granted.

EQUITY LOANS

An equity loan is used to release the equity a buyer has in his present property so he can purchase a new property before his present property sells. This is usually used when a prospect is transferred and needs to relocate his family before his present property is sold. It can be used, however, when dealing with a client moving across town or across the street. A bank will loan him this money on a commercial loan without any monthly payments as long as his property is listed for sale. Usually they try to limit the loan to 80% of the value of the buyer's present property, less commission and mortgage. He then can use this money as a down payment on a new home.

If he is not assuming a mortgage or paying the total purchase price out of the equity loan, the bank loaning on his equity usually likes to have the first mortgage loan on the new home. The equity loan business is getting more competitive, however, and many banks will tell you that they will make the equity loan no matter where you take the first mortgage. It is good business to have your client open his savings and checking accounts with the bank making an equity loan, thereby giving them an added incentive to make the loan. The notes on this type of loan are usually for one year with extensions available if the borrower's old home has not sold.

As an example, a new prospect contacts you about purchasing a home. He has been transferred into your community by his company and would like to move his family in as soon as possible. He has his home listed, but it has not sold yet. You find a suitable home for him and now must get him into it as soon as possible, even though all his money is tied up in the equity of his old home. You write the offer subject to whatever conventional financing your buyer needs, and then add the terms subject to an equity loan for an amount equal to the down payment required. After the offer is accepted, you take a copy of the offer with your buyer for a loan application. You tell the banker you need an equity loan until the buyer's present home sells. They make him a personal loan, possibly asking for a lien on the property for security, for six months with no monthly payments. When your client's old home sells, he pays off the equity loan with the proceeds from the closing. You have released his funds from one home so that he might purchase another.

I have used equity loans when the intention was not necessarily to sell the old property. Suppose, for example, you have a client who would like to buy a property that he intends to put right back on the market after some repairs or rezoning, but does not wish to pay out any cash. Get him an equity loan on a property that he already owns. When the newly purchased property sells, pay off the equity loan and take the property that you listed to secure the loan off the market. You have arranged 100% financing for your client on a property that might otherwise not have had good terms available.

I once had a client who wanted to buy a home across the street from her present property. She owed only about $3,000 on the home she owned and needed to keep her payments low. We borrowed enough money to assume the mortgage on the property she was buying by using an equity loan. When her home was sold, she took the remainder of the proceeds and applied it to the mortgage on her new home; the bank lowered the payments and allowed her to keep the loan at the rate of interest that she had assumed. If we had had to wait for her house to sell, the property would still not have been on the market. There was no way she could afford the payments on a blanket with the large balance and higher interest. It took the equity loan to make the transaction.

CHATTELS

When financing commercial property or investment property, chattel mortgages can be used for secondary financing. A chattel mortgage is a loan on fixtures or equipment used in the operation of a business. In the case of an investment property, if the building was furnished, it would be the furniture. This type of loan is usually for a relatively short period of time because of the depreciation of the security involved. Depending on the condition and type of security offered, you could be looking at anywhere from one to ten years for the maturity of such a loan. If a consideration has been made for equipment or fixtures in the purchase price, you will probably not be in a position to use a chattel mortgage as secondary financing because it will be necessary to borrow on it to get the original loan. Many times, though, when buying an apartment building, the furniture is not priced separately, nor considered by the lender placing a first mortgage on the property. Go to your local loan company and get a loan on the furniture for your buyer to use as a down payment on the building.

Two buyers once ran across a businessman who wanted to sell out his casket business. He agreed to sell the building and equipment for $100,000 with terms of $25,000 cash for the equipment and

$75,000 on contract for the building. The buyers went to the bank and borrowed the $25,000 for the equipment using the same for security. Since the equipment was well worth the $25,000, they were able to borrow the entire amount, and since it was not a real estate loan, the bank was not limited to an 80% loan. By separating the equipment and building, the entire business was sold for 25% down. By lowering the price on the equipment and adding the difference to the real estate, the buyers were able to borrow the down payment money and had a good-sized business without putting up a cent. Had the equipment been included in the contract, or had the buyers gone to the bank for a first mortgage and chattel, it would have been necessary for them to put at least 25% down in cash.

This reinforces a point I made earlier. Know what you have available *before* you ever write the offer or see the banker. If the transaction had been presented to the bank as a 100% loan on a commercial property, it would never have worked. By coming in the back door and asking for the chattel mortgage only, we were able to get what we wanted.

I once sold a farm on contract for $37,500 with $5,000 down. It was an excellent buy, but that did not help me get the down payment that was needed. My buyers were from a large city 60 miles away and owned an apartment building in that city. They had assumed the loan on the property when the previous owner went into default. Even though they owed on the building, they did not owe on the furniture. They went to see a loan officer with whom they had transacted considerable business in the past. He agreed to loan them $5,000 on the furniture, and we had the necessary down payment for the farm.

It was important that the loan company was familiar with my buyers. He knew them, so the condition of the furniture or the use made of it was secondary. It is always easier if the borrower can deal with someone with whom he has a record of good will. Borrowers are always looking for a way to loan to a good customer, and many times the security or reason for the loan is the only evidence to their superiors that they are protected.

Whenever you can keep the equipment, fixtures, or furniture out of the first mortgage, you have left yourself an avenue of financing. Even if you don't need it now, there may come a time when your clients will be glad to have them free and clear. Since savings and loans cannot loan on equipment or furniture, your only sources for this type of loan are banks, finance companies, personal lenders and lease companies. Check out these outlets to find the most aggressive and liberal company to do business with. I have also found that you can reduce the down payment needed on some commercial property by letting the buyer assume some liabilities that the seller intended to pay off. By including them in the purchase price, you can reduce the down payment by an amount equal to that assumed. Don't overlook any opportunity to help yourself and your clients out of a tight money situation.

SECONDARY MARKETS ARE ALWAYS AVAILABLE

Secondary financing can be the key to a salesperson earning more than an average income. If you can put a transaction together using secondary money outlets, you can increase your sales by two or three thousand dollars per year. In addition to generating new clients whom you will be able to help, you will save sales that you have already put the time and effort into. These are the ones a salesperson must learn to save. Your commission has been earned, but if you fail to get a closing, your time has been wasted. It's bad enough to pass up a sale because you don't know how to finance someone, but it's worse to lose a sale for the same reason. At least if you pass up a buyer, you have not taken anything out of your pocket; you just don't put anything in it. If you lose one that you have worked three weeks on, you have in essence thrown several hundred dollars into the trash can.

These markets have funds when primary lenders don't. I've never known the secondary market to be dry, because of the rates and the fact that many times you are dealing with the people involved in the transaction, such as the seller, contract holder, or relative of the buyer. In addition, outlets are always available because there are so many of them. Success with secondary financing is not dependent upon the availability of an outlet, but rather on your ability to be aggressive and imaginative.

CHAPTER ELEVEN

Multi-Method Financing
That Solves any Problem

Real estate financing offers an interesting and exciting advantage over financing available on any other commodity. Not only are the sources and types of purchase funds available limitless, but also you have the flexibility of being able to combine different methods of financing to secure all the funds needed. You don't have to depend on any one lender to give you a commitment large enough to complete the transaction. This chapter will show you how to profit from this unique opportunity by presenting you with ten examples of creative multi-method financing that solves any problem.

USING MORE THAN ONE FINANCING METHOD
TO CLOSE YOUR TRANSACTIONS

One reason that financing a particular prospect seems impossible to a real estate agent is that he or she looks at the transaction with single vision. He reviews the financing avenues available to him and attempts to find *one* that meets his client's needs. When no one outlet is available, he usually gives up.

To succeed at financing 100% of your real estate sales, however, you have to take a broader look at your resources and match up as many financing avenues as it takes to complete the package—whether that be one or five. Every method of financing offers you the flexibility of using other methods to close the transaction. Always look at each transaction with an open mind and an awareness of how you can combine different types of financing to raise the total funds needed.

On the following pages you are given ten case examples of creative financing used by real estate agents to earn a commission check. Armed with a working knowledge of how others have capitalized on the opportunities they were afforded to finance real estate, you can apply the same principles to your financing problems.

EXAMPLES OF TEN SALES THAT WERE CLOSED BY USING TWO OR MORE METHODS OF FINANCING TO SECURE ALL OF THE MORTGAGE MONEY THAT WAS NEEDED

Example One: Combining Two Conventional Loans and a Second Mortgage

I recently had a property listed and an offer from the owners on another home subject to the sale of their home. The listed property was a double wide mobile home on an acre in the country. Finding a buyer was not difficult since it was just what every young couple was looking for, but financing the offer was a different matter. Money was tight and the banks would not loan on a double wide and ground, and the buyers were young with only $1,000 to put down.

To build both the buyer's and the seller's confidence so they would stay with me while I secured the funds we needed, and to get a commitment on the major portion of the loan, I arranged for a mobile home loan with a major mortgage company from out of town that specialized in mobile homes. I now had 50% of the purchase price committed.

Next, I arranged for a real estate mortgage with a bank in the county that had a history of loaning on bare land. They agreed to loan 50% of the value of the land, and I had a commitment for another 25% of the purchase price. Deducting the $1,000 down payment, I arranged for the sellers to take the remainder of the purchase price on a second mortgage. By combining three methods of financing, I was able to close the loan and earn two commission checks.

Example Two: Using Pledges with Conventional Mortgages

Any time you are dealing with a savings and loan and your buyer is short of down payment money, the opportunity to use pledges exists. I have also used pledges many times to make up the difference in a low appraisal.

In one instance, the lender gave us an appraisal $3,000 lower than the price agreed upon. The seller would not agree to a reduced amount, but did agree to a pledge for the $3,000. The final figures are listed below so you can better see how a pledge can save a low appraisal.

Original Offer	$40,000
Buyer's Down Payment	$ 8,000
Original Mortgage Requested	$32,000
Appraisal	$37,000
Down Payment	$ 8,000
Loan	$29,000
Pledge by Sellers	$ 3,000
FINAL LOAN	$32,000

Example Three: Using all Avenues Available for Farm Financing

I once had buyers willing to purchase a small farm I had listed for $100,000. The seller was unwilling to help with the financing, and while the buyers had $15,000 from the sale of their home, they anticipated needing this amount for remodeling the farmhouse.

First, we got a commitment from the Federal Land Bank for $75,000. Using the equipment and livestock involved, we then secured a $10,000 loan from Production Credit. I was still $15,000 short for the remodeling the buyers insisted needed to be done. To cover this amount, I went to a local lender and arranged a $15,000 home improvement loan for the buyers. This allowed us to use their $15,000 in equity from their former home as a down payment.

Example Four: Putting a Package Together with VA, Blanket Financing and a Contract

Many times you will be presented with an opportunity to put several properties on the market at the same time that belong to the same seller. One Detroit agent, presented with this potential multi-commission-earning opportunity, kept an open mind and looked at every financing avenue available to him.

He had listed five apartment buildings belonging to the same owner—one for $30,000, two for $25,000, one for $23,500 and one for $21,000. The owner had mortgages totaling $42,400 on the properties, which had a total listing price of $124,500. He contacted an investor to whom he had previously sold property and encouraged him to make an offer on all five using the following financing terms:

Total Offering Price	$124,500
Property No. 1	35,000 on VA
Property Nos. 2, 3, 4	60,000 on a 75% mortgage
Property No. 5	Balance not financed, on Contract

Using the $35,000 VA and $60,000 loaned on the blanket, the seller received $95,000 cash less expenses and a $29,500 contract on the fifth property (to be discounted to $21,000 if paid off within 18 months).

By adjusting the selling price of each property, financing the more expensive property and selling the least expensive property on contract, he sold the buyer all five properties without a down payment, solved the seller's problems and earned himself $5,229 in commissions.

Example Five: Combining a Chattel Mortgage, Real Estate Mortgage, Commercial Note and Second Mortgage to Finance Commercial Property

One of the difficulties in financing commercial property for a buyer with a small down payment is that the selling price is based on many items, some of which are intangible or difficult to finance. For instance, a price is always established on good will, but good will cannot be financed. Inventory and supplies make up a portion of the purchase price, but these are extremely difficult to finance, especially in the food industry. Even when you have collateral such as real estate, equipment, or accounts receivable, the loan-to-value percentage will not exceed 75% for long-term loans.

The same factors that cause you difficulty when financing a commercial transaction can also be the factors that enable you to secure the required purchase funds, if you are creative enough to take advantage of them. The following example shows how a knowledgeable and industrious real estate agent can transform disadvantages into advantages.

One Florida real estate salesman secured 95% of the purchase price of a wholesale supply company by combining a chattel mortgage on the equipment, a real estate mortgage on the building and a second mortgage secured by both the building and the accounts receivable. He then convinced the seller to allow the buyer to assume the accounts payable, rather than the seller paying them off, which allowed the buyer to deduct credit for this amount from the purchase price. He also secured a commercial note for the buyer to use for operating capital and inventory purchase, using the inventory for collateral. The net result was that the seller received the same net amount at the closing and the buyer had purchased a complete, operating business without investing any of his own funds.

		Financing:	
Total Purchase Price:	$300,000		
Accounts Payable	$4,000	Real Estate (75% of appraised value):	$187,500
Total Net Before Selling Expenses	$296,000	Chattel Mortgage (5 yrs on equipment based on appraisal by supplier):	52,000
		Second Mortgage (Secured by Accounts Receivable and real estate):	41,500
		Commercial Note (Purchase inventory and operating capital):	15,000
		Total Financed:	$296,000
		Assumption of Accounts Payable:	4,000
			$300,000

Other avenues are available when financing real estate, depending on the buyer's and seller's situation. Often, the seller can take a note for the inventory or take a second mortgage from the buyer. He can also keep the accounts receivable, rather than include them in the purchase price, which will reduce the amount of funds you must secure.

The buyer can also secure purchase money through his personal real estate or other holdings, using blanket mortgages, second mortgages or equity loans.

How you structure the purchase and financing of commercial property will determine your eventual success or failure. Businesses offer three, four, five or more tangible assets, yet the purchase price will usually be one lump sum. By designating the percentage of purchase price for each aspect of the business before taking the transaction to a lender, you can place the values in the manner that does you the most good. This kind of juggling is essential to securing commercial purchase money.

Example Six: Secondary Money Markets With VA and FHA Financing

The versatility of VA and FHA financing can be increased even more by combining them with other financing avenues when additional funds are needed.

One example of this is with small acreage. VA and FHA will not place much value on any land over one acre. To alleviate this problem and to enable my buyer to purchase the property with little or no money down, I divided the property into separate transactions, placing as much value as possible on the improvements on one acre and selling the remaining acreage to the buyer on contract.

Using this same technique, you can finance a business if the building also offers residential possibilities, such as a store with apartments. By securing mortgage funds on the building with VA and FHA, you can pick up the remaining purchase money on a commercial note secured on the business's personal property. As long as you don't use the property covered by the VA or FHA loan for collateral, it is perfectly legal.

Example Seven: Making Wraparound Mortgages a Valuable Tool in Your Multi-Method Financing Efforts

Wraparound mortgages offer you a tremendous opportunity to increase your flexibility when financing real estate. Since the wraparound is normally held by the seller, it can be anything you need it to be.

Its use can be particularly effective if the seller has a low interest rate loan on his home. By securing a second or third mortgage for him and then giving the buyer a mortgage that encompasses all of these loans at the current interest rate, the seller can realize most of his equity and get a nice return on his lower interest rate. He does so by profiting between his first mortgage interest rate and the higher rate he is charging the buyer.

Since you are dealing directly with the seller, your buyer is not limited in the avenues he chooses to secure his down payment funds and there are no restrictions on what percentage of the purchase price must be put down. This means the avenues are wide open to your imagination.

Example Eight: Securing Blanket Mortgages for Bare Land,
Construction or Investment Property

Blanket mortgages can be used in conjunction with many other types of financing to reach your buyer's goal. I recently put together a transaction using the buyers' equity in their home, along with 5½ acres and a partially completed home on a blanket mortgage to allow them to purchase the acreage. I then arranged for a construction loan with no monthly payments for six months, so they could complete the house on the new property. We then put their first home on the market and sold it after the new home had been completed, paying off the blanket mortgage. The construction loan was then converted to an amortized mortgage. The buyers had purchased the land they wanted, built the home they wanted and still had the convenience of their other home while building, without being obligated for two payments.

I often use blanket mortgages for the purchase of investment or commercial or investment property. If the buyer's equity in his present property is not great enough to cover the entire transaction when combined with the value of the property being purchased, I arrange for a second mortgage from the seller or a lender for the balance.

Blanket mortgages give you the flexibility to do almost anything since you are using the equity of two properties. If plans for the blanket mortgage are short-term or if one of the properties offers an income, blanket mortgages tied in with second mortgages or construction loans can make your financing easy.

Example Nine: Utilizing Leases for Down Payment Funds
on Conventional Loans

Leases can serve two uses for you when financing real estate. The first situation that presents an opportunity for the use of a lease is securing down payment funds for the buyer. The following case is a perfect example of how a lease was used to arrange 100% financing on a business.

An Idaho broker had a restaurant listed and found a buyer willing to purchase the business. The buyer was a manager of a restaurant with ten years of experience in the field, but he did not have any capital for a down payment. The purchase price was $150,000 including equipment, building and inventory.

He arranged for a first mortgage on the building for $100,000. He then contacted an Iowa-based lease company and received a commitment from them to purchase the equipment from the seller for

$30,000 and to lease it back to the buyer. To complete the transaction, the seller agreed to a second mortgage on the remaining $20,000.

This use of leases in conjunction with first mortgages, second mortgages and notes can be used in any business involving equipment in the purchase price.

The second situation where leases can make a transaction work involves the real estate itself, in one of three ways.

1. If a property is leased to a AAA company, a lender will loan 100% of the purchase price if the lease is assigned for security.
2. A purchase-lease back can be used to raise capital for the seller or buyer and to give the buyer the security of a long-term tenant.
3. A lease can also be used to finance the construction of a building. For example, Person A owns a lot. Person B leases the lot and constructs a building on the lot. In return, Person A gives Person B free rent for ten years. Person B gives Person A title to the building in return for ten years of free rent.

Example Ten: Exchanging Real Estate with Multi-Method Financing Techniques

The most obvious advantage to exchanging real estate is the tax advantage offered both parties; however, other advantages exist for exchanges that present you with additional opportunities to earn commission checks. These opportunities may be present when you have a business, apartment building, or in the case of an older couple, a residential house for sale. You may have a buyer looking for a larger home and a seller looking for a smaller home. A seller of a business may be willing to take the buyer's home in exchange or partial exchange for his business, since a single-family home is easier to sell and finance than a business. Always be on the lookout for opportunities to earn two commissions through the use of exchanges.

The biggest advantage to exchanges from a financing point of view is that the equities involved are completely flexible, and each owner is able to refinance his property before trading it for the other. By refinancing the property and exchanging equities, you have provided your clients with a tax-free source of revenue.

If the trade or equity exchange is not identical in value, you have numerous financing possibilities available to make the transaction work. Below is an example of such an exchange:

PROPERTY A		PROPERTY B	
Sales Price	$50,000	Sales Price	$70,000
Mortgage Balance	23,000	Mortgage Balance	50,000
Equity	$27,000	Equity	$20,000

The owner of Property B secures a $40,000 mortgage on Property A and puts $10,000 down. The owner of Property A secures a $56,000 mortgage on Property B and puts $14,000 down. Owner A has new property and $13,000 cash, while Owner B has new property and $10,000 cash. To increase the financing possibilities or to reduce any capital gains tax for which the owner of Property B might be liable, you can adjust equities to reach the same result. If refinancing is not in the best interest of your clients, the use of second mortgages will fulfill your needs for release of equity.

KEEPING AN OPEN EYE AND AN OPEN MIND TO MULTI-METHOD FINANCING OPPORTUNITIES

Multi-method financing can solve almost any financing problems that your clients may have. If your buyers are short of down payment funds, the appraisal you receive is low or the property to be sold is unique, you can save the transaction *and* your commission check if you watch for opportunities to utilize an additional financing outlet. The biggest obstacle you have to overcome is yourself. If you can keep yourself from getting into a narrow rut searching for the solution in any *one* financing outlet, you have overcome the biggest hurdle to successful real estate financing. The possibilities available to you are limited only by your own imagination.

CHAPTER TWELVE

How to Use Financing to Attract Buyers and to Sell Real Estate

Financing is much more than simply a necessary evil required to collect a commission check. Approached properly, financing is a method of selling in itself. Using your financing skills alone, you can attract more clients than you've ever had before and put together transactions that sell themselves. Instead of approaching the financing segment of your transaction with trepidation, you should be ecstatic and confident. You have, for the first time in the transaction, reached the only step you can completely control. This chapter will show you how to capitalize on your financing ability and how to sell financing, not houses.

LOCATING PROSPECTS WHO BELIEVE THEY CANNOT GET FINANCING

I've never met a person who said, "I have no interest in owning real estate." I do get a lot of excuses, though. They range from, "We're saving for a home," to "I'm not sure how long I'll be in this area." More often than not, however, the prospect's response is, "I would love to buy a home or investment property, but I can't afford to."

Either way, all excuses narrow down to one: "I don't think I can buy a home under my present circumstances." Your prospects want to buy. They are willing to do what you tell them needs to be done. They are playing "hard to get" to save them the embarrassment of being told they can't qualify. Here is where you win them over. YOU have the ability to develop just the financing they need, regardless of their credentials, and you let them know it. Until now they have been afraid to reveal their real desires to anyone; but you have given them the assurance they need.

Where do you find these individuals? Everywhere! Apartment buildings, restaurants, gas stations, mobile home courts, wedding ads, in factories, laundromats, shopping centers, or simply walking down the street. Anyone who doesn't already own a home, and half of those who do, would like to buy a home or an investment property. All you have to do is bring up the subject of real estate, and let them know that you can put them into their dream home, and you have them hooked. Can you imagine anyone liking a landlord telling them what they can do and when they can do it, having no security or control over their own home or having a neighbor a foot and a half away? Of course not!

If you have doubts that clients are that easy to find, step out of your office right now and stop the first person you meet (assuming it isn't another salesperson on his way in). Start talking real estate, and regardless of the excuse you get, tell them about the new financing program you just developed that enables you to get anyone into a home. You'll have them eating out of your hand. It works better than all of the home advertising you could ever do.

ADVERTISING THAT WILL DRAW AN OVERWHELMING RESPONSE

The most successful advertising I've ever run advertised an ability to finance anyone. Right in the middle of our line ads we would run an ad promoting our financing ability and dispelling the myth many would-be buyers have about what it takes to buy a home. Here is an example of our financing ads:

FINANCING AVAILABLE: You can buy a house today, regardless of your circumstances. We have financed clients with credit problems, little or no money for down payments, buyers with moderate incomes, singles, widows, divorcees, retirees and even clients who had filed for bankruptcy. As financing experts, we have the ability and contacts to develop a financing program just for you using over 30 different methods of real estate financing. If you want a house, not excuses, call us right now at ....

Or

VETERANS — Did you know that — Your real estate eligibility *did not* run out with your other benefits — you can buy up to a $100,000 home without a down payment or even closing costs — that you can use your eligibility more than once — that you get special consideration from VA — that you can buy a farm or apartment building under VA? We know. Call us today for more details at ....

Or

$500 AND AN INCOME — If you have these two ingredients, we can help with the rest and put you into this sharp two-bedroom starter home. The owner will even pay all closing costs. If you've thought you couldn't buy a home because of the down payment, monthly payments or your credit, call us today and we'll make you a part of the home-owning community.

Or

IF YOU'VE BEEN TOLD "NO," YOU HAVEN'T TALKED TO US! We make our living succeeding where others fail. Take five minutes, right now, and call us at .... Our record of financing buyers proves that we can show you how to become a home owner, regardless of what others have told you.

Advertising such as this will draw a much larger response than any single ad on a home. You will be overrun with calls, and a majority of them will be from prospects who are really in much better shape than they realized. Most of the buying public has been brainwashed over the years to believe that you have to have several thousand dollars down or a large income to afford a home. You have to make them aware that this is no longer true, or they will quietly sit back and wait for years before attempting to buy a home.

MOST PEOPLE WILL BUY A HOME IF YOU CAN SHOW THEM HOW

Owning a home always has been and still is the American dream. Incompetent salespeople and fatalistic media coverage have made many potential buyers put their dream aside; but it is still there. Almost all nonhome owners under the age of 40 will buy a home, if you can show them how. The market hasn't slowed, only the salespeople. First-time home buyers don't care what the economy is like or the weather. They want a home and will buy the financing once you get it for them. In other words, first-time buyers are not looking for *the* home; they are looking for *a* home. They want something they can call their own, something to build on so they can reach their goal in the future. Buyers who believe they can't purchase a home with the assets they have will still have some basic requirements in a home, but if you can come close to their needs in size and neighborhood, they will buy what you can finance.

These buyers not only provide an opportunity for you, they are also a responsibility for you. Only you stand between them and their goal of owning a home. If you are not creative enough, industrious enough, persistent enough, they will not reach their goal. If you fail, they are likely to crawl back into their shell until a more competent agent appears to help them become homeowners. They will not venture out on their own for another rejection. This is your responsibility. Success means a commission check and future referrals for you, and happy homeowners who will remember you faithfully. Failure helps nobody. Only you can ensure success. Remember, thousands of prospects are just waiting for you to show them how to help you earn a commission check.

OVERCOMING YOUR BUYER'S FEARS

You have one major obstacle to overcome in succeeding at getting financing for your clients: their own fears. You can solve any problem your clients may have if you know the truth about their circumstances from the very beginning. Unfortunately, most prospects are afraid to tell you the truth for fear you will reject them or that the truth will stop them from getting a home. Using this logic, they decide that if the truth would prevent them from owning a home, their only alternative is to tell you what they think you want to hear. If the truth catches up with them, so what, they haven't lost anything. Of course, the problem with that logic is that if you know you have a problem, you can take steps to solve it or select a financing method that will succeed even with the problem.

Your first and most important step then is to encourage your prospects to be honest with you. You must accomplish this goal early, since once they have told you a lie, they cannot later admit the truth. To ensure that you do not put your clients in this corner, begin your presentation with a conversation designed to both put them at ease and give them confidence in their ability to buy a home.

"Mr. and Mrs. Prospect, the first thing I want to do is put you at ease. My job is not to approve or disapprove of your loan. I work for you and the seller and my only goal is to get you into a home you will enjoy. I can get you financed, regardless of your circumstances as long as I know what they are from the start. I have financed buyers who had filed for bankruptcy, had no money for a down payment, were new on a job and even buyers who were on social security. There are over 30 different financing programs and hundreds of homes on the market. In fact, I've never met a buyer who didn't have some problem we had to overcome. The idea that buyers have good credit, large down payments and substantial incomes just isn't true. Let's begin by discussing what you have to work with and what you're looking for in a home, and then I can tell you which method of financing we can use and what homes we should be looking at."

By telling your prospect that all buyers have some sort of problem and that you have the ability to finance them, regardless of their circumstances, and letting them know you want their financial information only to determine which method of financing to use and not to judge their ability to buy, you have removed the barriers and given them a respectable way to admit their problems. This is essential if you are to develop the relationship you need to complete the transaction. Explain to them how you can help and why it is important to know the facts *before* you show them homes or get an offer. You are concerned about them, you are going to help them and you are the expert. They will reveal the true picture to you, unless you make them feel they must meet some predetermined image of a buyer.

GENERATING COMMISSIONS WITH YOUR FINANCING ABILITY

If you get nothing else from this book, I will have succeeded if you realize just one thing. *Your financing ability doesn't just enable you to finance an offer so you can earn a commission: financing is a means of generating commissions.* Even if you have no prospects, you can make sales by seeking out those individuals who want to buy a house, but think they can't because of their credit, income or amount of cash available. I have financed hundreds of homes that were sold solely because either I or another agent said, "I can get you into this house with what you have to work with." It wasn't the best house. It wasn't even what they described as the house they wanted. But it was the house I could get on the terms they needed and that made them put their name on the bottom line.

I had a house listed that had excellent assumption terms, but was small and had only two bedrooms. My listing was about to expire and we hadn't been able to sell the home. It was in good condition and in a good neighborhood, but it was priced high since the seller had just recently purchased the home. I couldn't find a willing buyer. Finally, it occurred to me that I knew a man who had filed for bankruptcy because of a business failure and he had lost his home in the process. No lender would make him a loan, because it had only been a few months since his bankruptcy. He was also limited by the amount of down payment he could afford. I stopped by to see him and suggested that I could get him into a home and give him a chance to rebuild his credit.

The man was delighted by the prospect and made an offer on the property within two hours, even though he had to sell over half of his furniture so he could fit into the new home. Not only did I earn a commission just because of the financing I could offer him, but within three years inflation had increased his equity tenfold and with his credit history of paying on this home, I was able to sell him a beautiful home for three times the price of his first purchase. I earned two sales commissions and two listing commissions solely because I could offer a man financing on a home that he wasn't even in the market to buy.

PROFITABLE PROJECTS WHEN SALES ARE SLOW

You don't have to sell a house to earn commissions with your financing ability. Many people will pay you handsome fees for arranging financing for them for numerous reasons. One Indiana broker uses his creative financing techniques to boost his income during normally slow winter months. First, he reviews his records to see for whom he has sold property using contract terms. He then makes a tour of the lending institutions in the community to determine the names of all contract sellers who have escrow accounts with the lenders. After compiling his list of potential clients, he contacts the contract sellers and asks if they are interested in having the contract paid off so they can receive their equity. Of course, most of them are very interested. If they are, the broker signs an agreement with them that requires the contract seller to pay him a $200 fee if he can arrange for their contract to be paid off.

With his commission secure, he approaches the contract buyer and explains the advantages of getting a mortgage to pay off the contract holder. The buyer can get title to the property, will enjoy reduced taxes because he can file a mortgage exemption, and in many cases he is able to get the buyer a discount on the contract as an inducement to secure a mortgage. Not only do his efforts pay off in financing fees, but also he will often find that the contract buyer is interested in selling or in buying another home. His aggressiveness puts him into situations that create opportunities to earn commissions by listing or selling homes to his contacts.

This is just one example of how to use your knowledge of financing to earn additional income. Intrafamily transactions, businesses, refinancing for personal needs and for-sale-by-owners all present opportunities for you to solve someone's problems and earn yourself a commission besides.

DEVELOPING THE "NO COMPETITION" MARKET

Not only are the prospects with financing problems easy to sell, but they also offer the advantage of no competition for their business. Every salesperson in your community is competing for the buyer with a large down payment or substantial monthly income. You are constantly looking over your shoulder to see who is trying to steal your client now. These buyers, however, do not present you with that problem. The majority of your peers are not competing for them. They wouldn't know what to do with them if they had them for clients. They're still looking for the easy ones. The market is yours to develop.

A client who initially believes he can't be financed will also be extremely loyal to you. Last week the client knew he couldn't buy a house. Now, all of a sudden, you have given him hope. He is not about to take a chance on failure by switching agents now. Besides, he feels an obligation to you for solving his problem and enabling him to realize his dream.

To develop a "No Competition" clientele, all you have to do is listen to what your prospects are really saying. I've told you where to find them; now all you have to do is resist the urge to disregard their ability to buy. Work with them; show an interest in them. You will be the first salesperson to tell them you can help. They can buy a home. From that point on, they will be yours, unless you neglect them.

If a prospect is interested enough to call you on the phone or to tell you what he wants to do "some day," he can earn you a commission check and he is worthy of your time and efforts. While the rest of the agents in your city are out chasing the prospects who really don't need them, you'll have buyers coming to you who couldn't succeed without you.

SELLING AND FINANCING OTHER AGENTS' REJECTS

My biggest source of clients come from other agents. Their rejects and failures earn me more money than I could ever earn looking for the perfect client. I know I can finance anybody. The fact that another agent has told the client he can't buy a home because he doesn't qualify, makes my job easy. Once I show an interest in the buyer and assure him that I can get him financed and that I don't care what his problems are, I have a willing and loyal client.

Because of the actions and inabilities of other salespeople, these buyers will have been sold on the need to do exactly what you tell them needs to be done. They know they have no place else to turn and they have to pin their hopes on you. You have also demonstrated to them that you know what you are doing and that you're interested only in their welfare. Getting them to cooperate will be easy, and you owe it all to the agent who told them, "You can't qualify for a loan."

THE RETURN ON YOUR EFFORTS WILL BE MANIFOLD

Granted, the effort you must put forth to finance buyers with credit, income, or down payment problems will be greater than that you must exert for buyers with good credentials, but the rewards will also be greater. First, you have a loyal client, so you know you will be the one who earns a commission. Second, these types of buyers know others in the same position and they will happily recommend your services to their friends. I have found that they virtually go out looking for someone to refer to you, because they want others to share in the same happiness they have and they want to repay you for your efforts on their behalf. Third, they will remember you when it is time to sell and when they are ready to buy a new home. They know you can finance the buyer for their home, and they want to use an agent in whom they have confidence when they purchase their new home.

With rare exception, I receive referrals from difficult-to-finance buyers including their parents, brothers, sisters, friends, co-workers and even grandparents. Seldom do I earn less than four commissions as a result of my ability to finance someone who felt he couldn't buy a home. So, when I'm asked if my efforts are worthwhile for a $600 or $700 commission, my response is always the same, "No, they're worth four times that ... and that's what they'll earn me, too."

CHAPTER THIRTEEN

How and Where
to Find Money
for All of Your
Real Estate Needs

Now that you know about the major methods of financing real estate that are available to you, and have discovered how to create the financing you need to close a transaction, your only need is to locate the funds for the financing you develop. This chapter will show you where to find mortgage funds and give you examples of how other agents have used their ingenuity to locate new mortgage outlets.

CREDIT MAKES THE WORLD GO 'ROUND

We've all heard the old saying, "Love makes the world go 'round." Being a romanticist, I wouldn't find fault with that statement, but from a business standpoint, it might be more appropriate to say, "Credit makes the world go 'round." Thousands and thousands of institutions, employing hundreds of thousands of people, survive only if they loan money. Millions more depend on credit for their employment. Their employers must be able to obtain funds on reasonable terms for equipment and for operating capital. Consumers must be able to buy products on credit in order to create a demand for the goods manufactured. If a bank or savings and loan doesn't make numerous loans, they will have no way to pay overhead, employees' wages or interest to their depositors. Regardless of what they say, they have to loan money. When you think about it, the world would most surely "stop" without credit.

I point this out so you might better understand the strength of your position. The lenders need you and your borrower as much as you need them. Many lending officers will act as though they are doing you and your buyer a favor by granting your buyer a loan. Not so! You are doing the officer a favor by offering him your business, since you can take your business anywhere. Your relationship should be treated as a mutually beneficial transaction. Don't forget; you are providing an honest and needed service to buyer and lender alike.

You should let the lender know in a diplomatic way that you like doing business with him and you are pleased to bring your offers to him, but that you have many other outlets available to you. Through your confident style, you must communicate to the lender that you will favor him with your business as long as he appreciates it and works to get your loans approved. Otherwise, you will begin to look elsewhere for your mortgage funds.

LOOKING FARTHER THAN YOUR OWN BACK YARD

Too many real estate agents think that their only outlets for money are the banks and savings and loans in the community in which they are selling. There are many outlets for money, not only within the area, but all over the state and country. Banks and savings and loans in neighboring cities and counties, mortgage companies, lease companies and commercial banks would enthusiastically welcome your business, also. It would be unusual for a bank or savings and loan from a nearby city not to want to expand into your market. Mortgage companies may not have an office in your community, but they will send an officer to take your loan applications. Commercial banks and lease companies cannot do enough business to sustain themselves, unless they go out of their locale to do business.

Finding these outlets takes common sense and a little detective work. Your local abstract and title companies can give you information about lenders who have previously loaned in the area. Almost any franchise restaurant owner can give you the name of a lease company he has available to him. Pick up your phone and call any insurance company. If they don't finance property, they can tell you who does. If you're having trouble locating a mortgage company to do business with in your area, call FHA or VA to find out who has been processing loans with them. It won't hurt to pick a commercial bank in a large city at random. If they can't handle your loan, they will tell you who can. When you need private funds, or feel they are the best source to get what you need, place an ad in the paper. Call all the banks and savings and loans within a 20-mile radius to see if they want to get into your area. Almost any farmer can tell you where the nearest Federal Land Bank or Production Credit Office is located. A few hours at the courthouse will tell you which institutions and individuals now carry mortgages or liens in your area.

SOMEONE, SOMEWHERE WANTS TO LOAN YOUR CLIENT MONEY

The important thing to remember is that there is always someone, somewhere, who wants to loan money for what you need. Have you ever worked a hidden word game? The puzzle is a page full of letters, arranged in such a way as to hide the words you must find to win. At times it is difficult to find that final word or two you need to win. You wonder if they made a mistake and forgot to put them in, but quite honestly, you know they didn't, so you keep looking. You know the answer is there and you look until you find it. Financing is the same; the solution, the outlet, is always there. The successful salesperson is the one who keeps looking until he wins the game.

KNOWING YOUR LENDERS AND YOUR CLIENTS' NEEDS

While not getting it right the first time is not a fatal mistake, failing to properly consider your client's circumstances and needs with the policy of the lender you have chosen can cause unnecessary delays in closing and seriously damage your relationship with your buyer. Granted, matching up the right lender with the right transaction is not always easy considering the alternatives available to you, but if you really know your lenders, you will be able to quickly eliminate those that won't work for a particular buyer or home.

In determining which lender you should use, you must take into consideration every aspect of the transaction, including the property, the sellers, closing costs, closing time, your buyer's credit, income and down payment, secondary funds required, interest rates and terms offered, and the lender's policies and how they apply to your client. For instance, if you need a pledge, you know you can't use a bank, but if you need a second mortgage, a bank or finance company will be your best source. If the sellers need to close in two weeks, you must look at conventional or conventional insured mortgages, rather than VA or FHA, but if your buyer's credentials are questionable, FHA or VA may be the only outlet you have. Each transaction will require different considerations.

The most important point is to know the lender's policies and your client's credentials before you make the loan application. Visit each lender and discuss his policies in different circumstances. Invite a lending officer from a different institution to your sales meetings each week and give him "what if" examples so you can freely discuss problems without having before you an offer you need to get financed.

Most of all, be thoroughly prepared and never be caught unaware of a skeleton in your buyer's closet prior to or after a loan application. Research your clients before you take them for the loan application. After the lender discovers the problem, it will be too late to correct it.

FINANCING METHODS AND SOURCES LISTING

Below is a list of sources for mortgage and down payment money, as well as a list of the different types of financing available for mortgage and down payment purposes. Make a checklist of these and have it available when considering which avenue to pursue in obtaining funds for your clients.

TYPES OF FINANCING	SOURCES OF FUNDS
1. FHA 203B (Normal FHA)	1. Banks
2. VA	2. Savings and Loans
3. FHA–VA	3. Mortgage Companies
4. Farmers Home Administration	4. Finance Companies
5. 95% Insured	5. Credit Unions
6. 90% Insured	6. Pension Funds
7. Conventional Uninsured	7. Insurance Companies
8. Blanket Mortgage	8. Private Individuals

9. Package Mortgage
10. Equity Loan
11. Second Mortgage
12. Assumption
13. Contract
14. Farm Loans
15. Commercial Real Estate Loans
16. Pledge (Two Types)
17. FHA 221D2
18. FHA 222
19. FHA 235
20. FHA Multi-Unit Loans
21. Construction Loans
22. Balloon Payment Mortgages
23. Purchase-Lease
24. SBA
25. FHA 203 (New Home Loans)
26. VA New Home Loan
27. Chattel Mortgages
28. Purchase Money Mortgage (Owner-Finances)
29. Exchange
30. Notes (Commercial or Private)

9. Federal Government
10. Federal Land Bank
11. Mutual Funds
12. Commercial Banks
13. Contract Sellers
14. Sellers
15. Relatives
16. Lease Companies

I am always amazed when people tell me they can't find the money they need. If you will use this list, that should never be a problem for you.

OVER 30 METHODS OF FINANCING AND 16 SOURCES OF FUNDS CHARTED TO SHOW WHERE TO LOOK FOR DIFFERENT TYPES OF MORTGAGE MONEY

Below is a chart that combines the two lists above so that you can quickly and easily identify which types of mortgage loans are available from which types of lenders. This chart will also demonstrate to you the tremendous number of financing avenues available to you to secure your mortgage funds.

Places where money can be obtained

Types of Loans

	1	2	3	4	5	6	7	8	9	10	11	12	13	14	15	16
1	x	x	x						x							
2	x	x	x						x							
3	x	x	x						x							
4									x							
5	x	x	x													
6	x	x	x													
7	x	x		x	x			x							x	
8	x	x		x	x			x							x	
9	x			x											x	x
10	x			x				x							x	
11	x	x		x	x			x						x	x	
12	x	x	x	x	x			x						x	x	
13								x					x	x	x	
14	x	x					x	x	x	x			x		x	
15	x	x	x			x	x	x			x	x	x	x	x	
16		x					x			x				x	x	
17		x							x							
18		x							x							
19		x							x							
20		x														
21	x	x			x			x	x			x			x	
22	x	x				x	x	x			x	x	x	x	x	
23							x							x	x	x
24	x	x						x				x				
25	x	x	x						x							
26	x	x	x						x							
27	x			x		x		x				x	x		x	x
28														x		
29	x	x						x				x	x	x	x	
30	x			x	x		x	x				x	x	x	x	

SIX EXAMPLES OF REAL ESTATE AGENTS FINDING MORTGAGE MONEY IN UNUSUAL PLACES

To give you an even better idea of how limitless the sources available to you for real estate financing are, I have selected six examples of how creative real estate agents have not given up when the normal channels were closed to them. Their persistence and ingenuity earned them commissions that would have been lost by most real estate agents.

Example One

In attempting to arrange for the purchase and lease-back of equipment involved in the sale of a small Indiana tool company, I had to go to California to find a company willing to take the transaction. Through advertisements in a business publication, I ran across the names of several lease companies. On the first trip, I was successful in securing a lease agreement with a California firm.

After making the initial contact, I forwarded them my buyer's P & L, an itemized list of equipment and an appraisal on the equipment. After reviewing these documents, the lease company approved the purchase and lease-back of the equipment and the buyer and seller flew to California to complete the transaction. The closing was held within three weeks of my first contact with them with no more work involved than when financing a property through a local bank, even though the lender was 3,000 miles away.

Example Two

One of the most unusual loans arranged by an agent was a result of his contact with a pension fund administrator. He was searching for a first mortgage commitment during a period of tight money. Having been turned down by all the local lenders, he ran an ad in the newspaper soliciting private investors, pension funds, and treasurers of organizations to loan first mortgage money at a higher rate than was available on current long-term investments.

The next day he was contacted by the administrator for a newly-developed pension fund for a local union. The man had been trying to decide how to invest the pension funds in the most secure and highest yielding market. After the agent explained how the fund's money would be protected and showed him the yield available, the administrator agreed to take a look at the buyer's credentials.

Not only did he make the loan, but he was also offered an additional outlet for his mortgage needs; he could submit his future applications to the investment committee of the pension fund. What made the transaction possible was the agent's planting of the idea in the mind of the administrator through his newspaper ad. Since you don't know every possible lender or investor, advertising is an excellent way to attract new outlets for financing your real estate sales.

Example Three

I had an historic property for sale that was very attractive to history buffs, but not to banks. Securing an offer was not difficult, but none of the local banks wanted to loan over 50% on the property, since the resale market was limited. The home was in bad need of repair, which concerned most lenders, also.

As a last resort, we submitted a loan application to the credit union where the buyer was employed. Surprisingly, the loan was approved for 80% of the purchase price. Credit unions, I have found, are more liberal than most lenders because they are closely associated with the borrower and they deduct the loan payments directly from the employee's paycheck. With this added assurance of getting their money every month, the most important criterion is the employee's seniority in his company.

Example Four

An agent from Tulsa, Oklahoma, related his success to me in securing financing from the holders of land contracts. Faced with the problem of not being able to secure a reasonable mortgage on a property because of its location and condition, and unable to sell the property on contract (since the present owner was buying the property on contract), John turned to the original contract seller to solve his financing needs.

The owner owed a balance of $18,000 on a contract at 8% interest. With a $27,000 sales price, he had $9,000 equity in the property. The buyer had $3,000 to put down and there was no suitable method of securing conventional mortgage funds.

The contract seller owed only $5,500 on the property at an interest rate of 7½%. John convinced the contract holder to secure a second mortgage on the property for $6,000 and to give $6,000 to the owner, along with the buyer's $3,000 down payment. The owner then released all interest in the property, turning his interest back over to the contract holder. A new contract was signed between the original contract seller and the new buyer for $24,000 at 13% interest.

The owner received his equity and while the contract seller did not increase his equity, he increased his interest return from 8% to 13% without losing any equity or investing any cash. John has since used this method several times to sell property already financed on contract.

Example Five

Out-of-town banks are seldom thought of as outlets for real estate mortgages, but often they are more effective than the local lenders. I have arranged for mortgages from other counties, the state capital and even from different states. If you select your outlets wisely, you will discover that many have more money than they can disburse in their own communities; and if they are in neighboring counties or cities, you'll find a desire to expand into a competitor's territory.

The courthouse records in my county are witness to this fact. In one afternoon I found mortgages to lenders in Henry County, Fayette County, Randolph County, Indianapolis, Dayton, Cincinnati, Louisville, Detroit, seven counties in Ohio, Chicago, New York, and Los Angeles. These unusual outlets were uncovered in one single four-hour period in a relatively small courthouse.

Using the logic that if they loaned on property in this area once, they would loan again, I have used many of these lenders to finance property when the local lenders were reluctant to issue a commitment on an application. In one year, I secured 37 mortgages through out of town lenders. Because of my efforts to attract out-of-town lenders, I helped agents earn 37 commission checks in one year that would have otherwise been lost.

Example Six

Private investors are good outlets for mortgage funds if you know how to develop them. Below is an example of how one agent solicited private investors to raise mortgage funds for her buyer.

First, she ran an ad in the local paper offering the current rate and points for mortgage money. Her cost for a weekly line ad was about $12.

Next, she reviewed business publications and selected three to run monthly ads in, again offering the current interest rate for first and second mortgages. She also used these same periodicals to extract ads placed by investors and contacted each one to verify terms and rates. Her costs for the ads totaled $74 per month.

The results were very productive. In the first month she received commitments on three transactions she had been trying to finance, earning her a total of $2,894 in commissions.

Now, each month she is in contact with private investors willing to provide her mortgage funds for her real estate sales. For a $122 per month investment, she has her own private source of mortgage funds that is limited only by the number of properties she can sell.

LOAN REJECTIONS ARE YOUR FAULT, NOT THE BUYER'S

The real estate industry has become too competitive to make the buyer responsible for bringing you credentials that will make your job easy. Today, if you have a client who wants to purchase a home, you must take the initiative to find financing that meets his abilities. You are the expert and you are also the one who will not earn a living if the transaction does not close. No one is responsible to see that you earn a living except you. No one is going to see that you earn a living except YOU.

It may soothe your ego to blame a loan rejection on your buyer, but it doesn't put any money into your pocket, and we both know that all buyers can be financed one way or another. So your excuses are only for your spouse and your broker. Ultimately, we must take responsibility for our own failures. Then and only then can we correct the problem and see that it doesn't happen again. In fact, once you realize that the rejection was your fault and not the buyer's, you will probably jump in your car and go get another offer from him, so you can do it right this time. After all, as in canvassing, each rejection just puts you one step closer to an acceptance.

Index